Rector Transitions:
A Handbook for
Episcopal Lay Leaders

Van Sheets

VTS PRESS

First Published in the United States by

VTS Press
Virginia Theological Seminary
3737 Seminary Road
Alexandria, VA 22304
www.vts.edu

Cover art courtesy of
Saint Michael and All Angels Church – Dallas
Used With Permission

ISBN-13: 978-0692125137

ISBN-10: 0692125132

Printed in the United States of America
September 2018

FIRST EDITION

Contents

Toolbox

Foreword

"TEACH ME DISCERNMENT AND KNOWLEDGE..." Psalm 119:66

Life is a series of endings and beginnings. And each is accompanied by a time or a season of transition. "Our days are like the grass," the Psalmist tells us, "we flourish like a flower of the field; when the wind goes over it, it is gone, and its place shall know it no more. But the merciful goodness of the Lord endures for ever..." Again and again things that seem permanent and dependable in our lives are tossed about by the winds of change. This is true of our relationships, our work, and the sum of our days. Some transitions are extremely painful and involve profound loss: the death of a loved one, our good health, a position, a home, a homeland, a sense of one's worth. Other transitions we embrace gladly: a commitment to share our life with a beloved, the birth of a child, a new job, a new house, and a promotion. Yet, even the transitions we welcome contain within them a loss of the familiar and a season of disorientation as we adjust to what is new. Change, observed the philosopher Eric Hoffer, even when it is positive, is an experience of loss. For a congregation, the ending of a pastoral relationship and the intervening season before a new pastor is chosen can be a time of loss and disorientation. Acknowledging these feelings, and situating them within a context of prayer, can lessen anxiety and help a congregation prepare for what lies ahead.

A PRAYER IN A TIME OF TRANSITION

God of all ages and keeper of our days,

We lay before you this season in which we find ourselves.

What has been has ended

and we know not what lies ahead.

Be with us in this time

and give us the courage and patience to live these days

of losing and finding

mindful, as Jesus taught his friends,

that the grain of wheat must be planted in the earth and die

in order to bear much fruit. Amen.

All along life's way we are confronted by choices. This route or that? Yes or no? Now or later, or perhaps never? Making choices involves discernment and examining the pros and cons of our possible responses. Here I am put in mind of the counsel in the First Letter of John to "test the spirits." This means that as we make decisions, particularly when they are far-reaching, we must do so from a stance of awareness. We must go below the surface of our thoughts and examine what lies behind our attitudes and perceptions. We must acknowledge the various preconceptions and biases, "the spirits," that color our thinking and our responses to others and the world around us. Even when confronted by unforeseen and difficult circumstances, we have the freedom to choose how we will dispose our hearts. We can choose the *spirit* in which we will receive what has been given to us.

"The Lord knows the thoughts and intentions of our hearts. Without a doubt, every one of them is known to him, while we know only those that he lets us read by the grace of discernment," writes Baldwin, a 12th century Archbishop of Canterbury. "Our spirit does not know all that is in us, nor all the thoughts which we have, willingly or unwillingly. We do not always perceive our thoughts as they really are. Having clouded vision, we do not discern them clearly with the mind's eye."

Baldwin's words are as true now as they were in his own day. Clouded vision is common to us all. And, therefore, when we are seeking to accord our desire with God's desire, as in discerning a new priest and pastor, being aware of "the spirits" present in our thoughts and feelings helps us to have a greater degree of spiritual freedom and unclouded vision as we undertake this sacred task.

Engaging with others in a process of discernment quickly brings out of hiding our various contrary attitudes and opinions. Our temperaments, life experiences and what we each consider normative may be challenged. We may quickly discover that such moments are invitations to enlarge our vision and make room for God's mysterious ways, which transcend the limits of our individual desires.

In the pages that follow, Van Sheets sets out in principle and detail what practicing discernment entails when undertaken by faithful members of a congregation intent upon grounding their personal and collective vision in the larger vision of God's will as they seek new clerical leadership. Nothing here is untested. Everything grows out of the experience of the men and women who served on a discernment committee of which Van Sheets was co-chair. In addition to being a practical guide, this handbook provides a "Toolbox" of additional resources that proved useful in preparing and equipping the committee for its work, and is designed to help others embarking on that task. As the author makes clear, though the handbook can be adapted to any congregation, the fundamental steps remain the same.

Undergirding everything is prayer. Discernment is an intensely spiritual practice and must be grounded in prayer. With that in mind, I conclude with another prayer.

A PRAYER IN TIME OF DISCERNMENT

Holy Spirit,

You search us out and know us

better than we know ourselves.

All our thoughts and ways lie open before you.

Set us free from opinions and perceptions

that bind and imprison us.

Give us minds and hearts

ready to be lead in our discernment into the way of truth.

This we pray in the name of the One who is the truth,

who declares you the Spirit of truth,

Our Savior, Jesus Christ. Amen.

Frank T. Griswold

Introduction

One night the week before I finished writing this, our neighbors' home caught fire. The family escaped but their house was destroyed, leaving the brick outer walls and remnants of rooms. As the fire trucks left and the morning light rose, I joined the clump of people in the front yard. I asked where the mom was, and someone pointed through the front doorway to where she was looking for possessions that had survived. She trudged out into the yard holding a single item, a slightly charred wooden altar cross.

She slumped hard, too emotional to go back inside. Through the day we friends and neighbors searched through the soggy rubble for family mementos and other things that could be salvaged. Near the door to the back garden I noticed a wooden plaque, engraved and painted colorfully under a film of soot. It read, "Bloom where you are planted." I would have hardly noticed the plaque in a store, but in that moment it reminded me that every task is an opportunity to do something special.

If you are reading this, you are probably planted in a rector transition, or expect to be. It will have an enormous effect on your church's future and on you.

Listening to God's will is the central work of a rector transition, both for a congregation and for candidates considering the possible next stage in ordained ministry. Approach your transition faithfully and prayerfully. This is more important than any advice in this book or elsewhere.

A church's ministries result from a partnership between the clergy and laity. This book is for lay leaders, including the vestry, who lead a church through a transition and the search committee who seek God's guidance on behalf of the congregation. This lay leadership sets the foundation for the partnership with the next rector. Much of the book applies to all of your lay leaders. The sections on spiritual discernment and communicating with rector candidates are for the search committee.

Your church is unique. You must individualize your transition process, drawing on general guidance where you find it. This book grew from my experience on my church's search committee and reflects a portion of what we learned together. The Toolbox at the end of the book contains twenty-two worksheets and other tools you can adapt to your situation. These items are also available to download in digital format, at www.RectorTransitions.com. Churches of all sizes need to work through most of the transition steps, although some of the tasks are greater and more time-consuming for larger churches.

It is human to feel disoriented or even fearful upon entering a rector transition; if anyone tells you not to expect the transition to mean hard work, please ask him or her to send me examples of highly successful transitions that were easy. The transition is foremost a chance to achieve more of the great potential of your church. Pray for faith and energy. Be grateful for and embrace this opportunity for your church. A leadership transition resets a church's trajectory, either up or down. You can influence the power of your church's ministries for many years, and giving your best to this task will be one of the most rewarding and consequential experiences of your life. Godspeed.

Start Prayerfully

Before he taught and healed, Jesus did not make lists and create file labels. He prayed. Jesus set the example before he called the Twelve. "Now during those days he went out to the mountain to pray; and he spent the night in prayer to God."[1]

Praying together about your mission will unite search leaders and the congregation in working for the best possible results for your church. If you have a particular role in the transition, pause regularly, alone and with others, to pray and to listen to God's call for your church.

A rector transition is a communal faith journey, and many churches in transition find it valuable to choose or write a special prayer for use by the search committee and the congregation. You may have favorite prayers already that you could use. The Book of Common Prayer offers prayers that fit rector transitions, particularly on pages 816-18 and 832. If you choose to write your own prayer, you could develop ideas for it by asking each other questions such as, "What drew you to our church and continues to nourish you?" and "What do you dream for our future together?"

As we started, our committee developed a prayer for the church's transition. We kept it by our bedsides, we prayed it together at the end of every committee meeting, and the congregation prayed it as part of every worship service during the entire rector search.

We have a chapel where parishioners come to pray privately during the week, so we added a prayer station where people could light a candle and pray for the transition. I visited the chapel late one evening during a stressful moment in our search. As I came into the dimly lit chapel and saw flickering candles other parishioners had lit earlier in the day, I was instantly calmed and uplifted.

We placed take-away cards printed with the transition prayer at the prayer station. We also kept a book where parishioners could sign in or write a note. We made the sign-in book a gift to the new rector when he joined our church.

A search committee should establish a norm of praying during meetings, including stopping for prayer when there are anxious or tense moments during a discussion. At many moments our committee recalled a prediction from Brother Curtis Almquist, S.S.J.E., who has counseled numerous churches in discernment. "The weight of the task

---

[1] Luke 6:12. Unless otherwise noted, all quotations from the Bible are taken from *The New Revised Standard Version*.

will keep you on your knees."[2] Here are two well-known prayers that were favorites of our committee.

Teilhard de Chardin's Prayer

Above all, trust in the slow work of God.
We are quite naturally impatient in everything
to reach the end without delay.
We should like to skip the intermediate stages.
We are impatient of being on the way to something
unknown, something new.
And yet it is the law of all progress
that it is made by passing through
some stages of instability—
and that it may take a very long time.

And so I think it is with you;
your ideas mature gradually—let them grow,
let them shape themselves, without undue haste.
Don't try to force them on,
as though you could be today what time
(that is to say, grace and circumstances
acting on your own good will)
will make of you tomorrow.

Only God could say what this new spirit
gradually forming within you will be.
Give Our Lord the benefit of believing
that his hand is leading you,
and accept the anxiety of feeling yourself
in suspense and incomplete.

Pierre Teilhard de Chardin, S.J. (1881 – 1955)

---

[2] Almquist, S.S.J.E., in discussion with the author, April 2015.

Merton's Prayer

My Lord God, I have no idea where I am going.
I do not see the road ahead of me.
I cannot know for certain where it will end.
Nor do I really know myself, and the fact that
I think I am following Your will does not mean that I am
actually doing so. But I believe that the desire to please You
does in fact please You.
And I hope I have that desire in all that I am doing.
I hope that I will never do anything apart from that desire.
And I know that, if I do this, You will lead me by the right road,
though I may know nothing about it.
Therefore I will trust You always though I may seem to be lost
and in the shadow of death.
I will not fear, for You are ever with me,
and You will never leave me to face my perils alone.

Thomas Merton, O.C.S.O. (1915 – 1968)

Understand Congregational Transitions

Your church's internal and outreach ministries, evangelism, membership, and participation will be determined by the partnerships between the congregation and your successive rectors. Your history and lore contribute to how your church pursues ministry, as your community environment determines opportunities and constraints. Your partnership with the next rector will determine how you address challenges and how you choose opportunities to pursue.

A Spiritual Call

In the Episcopal tradition, rector transitions emphasize spiritual calls. The congregation listens for God's call regarding their future and seeks God's guidance before calling a rector. Candidates listen to God's call regarding whether they stay in their current roles or accept the possibility of a call from the transitioning church.

Some have observed that the common terms "rector search" and "search committee" imply that we are conducting a corporate-style recruiting process more than listening to God's call. They recommend we refer to "discernment committees" or "calling committees" to help remind ourselves that this is quite different from an executive search by a corporation. Others note that the transition process begins before the outgoing rector departs and continues until the new rector is fully integrated into the congregation in partnership with the laity. Whatever you name your committee, emphasize the spiritual nature of its work. I use the term "search committee" here only out of familiarity.

Think about Pastoral Transitions Systemically

A rector transition has three stages. You must accomplish each prayerfully and well to achieve the goal of leading your church to a fruitful partnership with your next rector and vibrant ministries in the future. The Ending Stage calls for saying good-bye to your outgoing rector and your church's past. The In-between Stage is a period for reflecting on your strengths, for imagining your future, and for seeking a new rector. The New Beginning Stage is a time of renewal and of forming the partnership with your new rector.[3]

The overall rector transition process is much the same regardless of church size. The steps in a successful transition take more hours for larger churches, but few of the steps can be completely skipped by a smaller church without making its transition less successful than it could be.

In transitions, priests need to focus on leaving well and starting well. Bishops must support diverse churches through all three stages. As a lay leader, you must lead your church energetically through each stage.

Search: The Pastoral Search Committee Handbook by the Rev. William Vanderbloemen, a Presbyterian pastor and founder of a search firm focused on leadership searches for denominational and unaffiliated churches, summarizes three general situations regarding the departure of the outgoing senior minister.[4] These scenarios are Emergency and Unforeseen Departure, Unforeseen but Unsurprising Departure, and Retirement.

---

[3] Different writers use various terms for the three stages of transitions. I borrow these terms from Sweetser, SJ, and McKinney, OSB, *Changing Pastors.*

[4] Vanderbloemen, *Search,* 17.

According to Vanderbloemen, the most common causes of emergency and unforeseen departures are moral failure, sickness, and unexpected death. If a congregation experiences one of these events, it should seek closure, with help from outside experts, before calling the next pastor. In the instances of sickness or death, this closure will require grieving as well as special support for the staff. In the case of moral failure, the church leadership should consider a review of its policies and procedures, and may need to address emotional fallout in the congregation.

Reasons for an unforeseen but unsurprising departure are less dire and could include a pastor's call to another church, stagnant growth, or leadership conflict. In these situations good communication is critical, and it is important to appreciate and celebrate the best of the recent era. If the underlying cause involves conflict, the congregation will need to work through the issues aided by transparent leadership and, in some cases, support from outside experts.

Retirement calls for celebrating the outgoing pastor's ministry and legacy, but Vanderbloemen warns against aggrandizement that could create problems finding a successor and building a good partnership with him or her. Thorough and coordinated communications during a rector's retirement pave the way for a smooth departure.

Beyond the "how to" focus of this handbook, I include a few observations to encourage you to think generally about Episcopal rector transitions. Given that the average tenure of a rector across The Episcopal Church is slightly over seven years,[5] I conservatively estimate that over 15 percent of parishes are in some stage of transition at any given time.[6]

Resources on Pastoral Transitions

This handbook grew from my experience as one my church's co-chairs of a rector transition in 2015-16. Early in our transition we explored written sources and interviewed leaders of our church's rector transitions during the past forty years, as well as experts across The Episcopal Church and other churches. Most of the advice

---

[5] Dr. Matthew Price (Senior Vice President for Research and Data, Church Pension Group), in discussion with the author, October 2015.

[6] If the average Ending Stage lasts three months, the average interim and search stage is six months, and the average time to integrate a new rector is six months, the calculation would be $(3+6+6)/(7 \times 12)+6 = 16.7\%$. In fact for many church transitions all three stages are longer than this example, and there are parishes that have spent more than a quarter of the past twenty years in some stage of rector transition.

was valuable. Some was inapplicable, a little was misguided, and some good information was hard to find.

Many dioceses provide written guides for parishes in transition. Some of these emphasize the spiritual discernment that is core to a congregation's call of a pastor, and some reflect valuable lessons the diocese has learned from both successful and unsuccessful parish transitions. However, most are written by clergy and, perhaps unintentionally, reflect a bias toward clergy-dominated leadership rather than lay-clergy partnerships in ministry. With this handbook I try to be comprehensive and practical from the perspective of lay leaders who aim for a vibrant ministry partnership with their rectors.

There are a number of books about pastoral transitions. Three sources have been most thought provoking for me:

Changing Pastors: A Resource for Pastoral Transitions is by the Rev. Thomas P. Sweetser, S.J., and the late Mary Benet McKinney, O.S.B. Sweetser is a Jesuit priest and consultant to Roman Catholic parishes. McKinney was a Benedictine sister who wrote and spoke widely on the subject of spiritual discernment. They collaborated with several Roman Catholic dioceses on a successful project to engage lay leaders more deeply in pastoral transitions. Some of the processes they described do not translate to The Episcopal Church, but they wrote wisely on spiritual discernment and transitions in pastoral relationships, which are far more important than the process mechanics.

A Change of Pastors, by the late Rev. Loren B. Mead, reflects the wisdom acquired from his experience working with hundreds of churches. Mead founded The Alban Institute, which from the early 1970s to 2014 consulted with churches, provided church education and training, led church research projects, and published on many subjects, including church transitions. From 1969 to 1974 Mead led a major study of the life of Episcopal congregations, and concluded, "Quickly we discovered the issue we had to deal with in every congregation was the relationship between the clergy and the lay leaders of that congregation."[7] Regarding pastoral transitions he wrote to lay leaders, "You are not in a 'hiring process.' You are in a transformation process. You will be transformed and your new pastor will be transformed."[8]

---

[7] Mead, *Change of Pastors*, viii.

[8] Mead, 60.

The Rev. Roy M. Oswald wrote more than twenty books that address the partnership between pastor and congregation, such as *New Beginnings: A Pastorate Start Up Workbook*. Oswald was an Alban Institute consultant for thirty-one years and retired in late 2015 as Executive Director of the Center for Emotional Intelligence & Human Relations Skills.

The web is full of resources about pastoral transitions, although some are not well curated. The Office for Transition Ministry (the "OTM") section of The Episcopal Church website[9] offers some useful materials, including the business-like guidebook written in 1985 by the Rev. Charles R. Wilson, *Search: A manual for those called to guide the parish through a process leading to the election of a rector*. The Episcopal Church Foundation Vital Practices website is another valuable resource as is Rev. Lindsay Hardin Freeman's compilation, *Doing Holy Business: The Best of Vestry Papers*. I mention other resources on specific subjects throughout this handbook and cite them in the bibliography.

Different denominations' transition processes incorporate the concept of calls differently. Writings on pastoral transitions strain when they aim broadly across denominations, but all the sources I mention have valuable insights for an Episcopal transition.

Participants in the Transition

This section introduces key roles in a rector transition and presumes your process is lay-led and aiming for a strong partnership in ministry with your next rector. Key participants include your bishop, whose counsel you should engage at the outset, and your outgoing rector, who has a special role that is discussed in the next section.

Vestry

Vestry members must understand the transition process in order to fulfill their leadership through the transition. Your vestry will issue the formal call to your next rector and approve his or her terms of employment.[10] The vestry establishes the search committee and delegates tasks to it. Your church and transition are unique, so I

---

[9] "Transition Ministry," *The Episcopal Church*, www.episcopalchurch.org/transition-ministry.

[10] Title III, Canon 9: "Of the Life and Work of Priests," of The Constitution and Canons of The Episcopal Church, addresses this in its Sections 3, 5, and 6.

address transition tasks without always recommending how you should share the tasks among the vestry, search committee, and possibly others.

Should vestry members serve on the search committee? This is a practical option in small churches with only a handful of leaders, but for churches with more lay leaders, it is better to minimize the overlap. In their roles as spiritual and temporal leaders of the church, vestry members need to be open and transparent with the congregation on almost all matters. As such, the culture and practices of a good vestry are antithetical to the confidentiality a search committee must maintain regarding the names of candidates and the communications with them.

There is also the practical matter of workload. Vestries assume more duties during an interim between rectors, and a rector search takes many hours and days. It could severely stretch part-time volunteers to serve in both roles.

It is important, however, that the vestry and search committee stay coordinated. They can work together on understanding the state of the church as discussed below. The search committee should give the vestry regular progress reports without naming candidates. Some churches designate one or two vestry members to serve as ex-officio search committee members to help the vestry and committee stay in sync.

Your rector transition likely will cross your vestry election cycle, so plan for how your vestry will stay apprised of the search and how you will orient newly elected vestry members during the transition.

Pay special attention to senior warden stability through your transition. Under the canons of The Episcopal Church and of many dioceses, the senior warden has canonical responsibilities that the rector would have in other years, such as hiring and firing staff. Check your diocesan canons and your church's Articles of Incorporation or equivalent formation documents to determine how you can ensure senior warden stability.

Perhaps the biggest question about the committee's assignment is whether the vestry directs it to bring them one recommendation or two to three finalists. I believe that in 99.99 percent of circumstances the committee should propose one final candidate to the vestry, and that proposing more than one is irresponsible because of the nature of a spiritual call discerned in community.

The committee is better placed than the vestry is to get to know multiple candidates through a thoughtful, integrated, and spiritual process lasting several months or longer. They will bond as a team and listen together to God's call for the church. The vestry cannot replicate the intensive, spiritual, and mutual discernment process that the committee shares with the candidates. Certainly they cannot know the candidates better from a few hours in a group or a series of one-on-one interviews. If your vestry feels it needs to meet multiple candidates, you should question whether something seems wrong with the search committee or the vestry or the discernment process.

Many churches have lost one or more final candidates in the sensitive final weeks of the courtship and have had to start over. Dividing the discernment process into search committee stage and a vestry stage increases the risks of misunderstandings that can cause a breakup. Candidates may view a divided discernment process as a red flag about church leadership. A divided process also increases the risk of a breach of confidentiality, which itself could deter some priests from entering discernment with the church. If you are not yet convinced, please circle back to this section after reading the rest of the handbook.

"Search" Committee

The most important task of the preparation stage of the transition is to form a good committee that will try to discern God's will on behalf of the congregation. Whatever you call your committee, recognize that the main work the vestry will assign it to do is spiritual, and select the committee prayerfully.

Every member of the committee should be faithful, able to collaborate deeply, and open to surprise in discerning God's will for your church. Every member should project joy and confidence. They should have diverse experiences in life and church, in personalities, and in how they relate to others. The committee should represent the diversity of the congregation. This does not mean each member represents a constituency, but that as a whole the committee should understand the varied perspectives of the congregation.

Aim for the smallest possible committee in light of the size of your church and the size of your search. A large church needs more committee members to understand the broad range of church ministries and to communicate with a larger number of parishioners. A search that includes more candidates has many more hours of work to share. Having more members, however, makes it harder to schedule meetings and share communications. More importantly, it adds to the time required to build the personal relationships of trust and appreciation for each member's wisdom, on which the discernment depends, because a larger group contains more one-on-one relationships.[11]

Your vestry will develop a list of prospective search committee members and address the challenge of assembling the smallest number of people with the greatest possible representation of qualities you want on your committee. Some articles about pastoral searches recommend selecting a committee based on complementary skills such as organization, writing, and interviewing. I disagree. Skills matter but are secondary to qualities that affect spiritual discernment and congregational leadership.

Romans 12 could be named the "Letter of Paul to Vestries and Search Committees in Rector Transitions." Paul began by exhorting the Romans to holy living and stressed that the body of Christ needs members with diverse gifts, all necessary and none elevated over others. He continued with instructions on how to be the church in the world. He wrote, "Do not be conformed to this world, but be transformed by the renewing of your minds, so that you may discern what is the will of God – what is good and acceptable and perfect."[12] It seems as if Paul were writing directly to discernment committees.

Before you form a search or call committee, read the sections below on how the committee prepares for and pursues spiritual discernment. Then compare prospective members to the characteristics you decide your committee needs. It helps to categorize the characteristics such as "Every member must have," "Some member must have," or "Helpful if some member has." Your committee does not necessarily need to be representative of your congregation demographically, socially, politically, or otherwise, but do be aware that your candidates will gain their impressions of your whole congregation from getting to know these people. **Tool 1** in the Toolbox at the end of the handbook is a worksheet to help form a search committee.

The search and discernment process is intellectually and emotionally demanding. The Rev. Elizabeth Rankin Geitz, who participated in many church transitions as Canon for Ministry Development and Deployment in the Diocese of New Jersey, recommends that lay leaders who are in major personal transitions may not want to help lead a church

---

[11] For example, a group of eight has twenty-eight different one-on-one relationships, whereas a group of eighteen has 153 different relationships. It takes larger groups more time and effort to build trust and mutual understanding.

[12] Romans 12:2.

transition, because the personal transition would "affect how (they) feel and react to the ups and downs of the Discernment Process."[13]

It is most common for a search committee to have <u>one chairperson</u>. My church's tradition is to have female and male co-chairs. My co-chair is such an exceptional leader and delightful friend that I now see this as the optimal way to share the workload and enhance leadership. It made our process thorough and avoided delays that could occur when a single chair's calendar becomes a bottleneck for the whole committee. Having co-chairs requires that they work together with complete trust and with a calendar handy.

Be sure prospective committee members understand the process they are committing to lead. It can <u>require many hours</u>, and a <u>completion date is unknown until late in the process</u>. The time required of the chair or co-chairs is particularly significant. Our large church's transition required more work than most, and we co-chairs each typically devoted twenty hours per week and sometimes more.

The vestry should charge the search committee formally by stating its expectations of the committee and then documenting those expectations in the vestry minutes. This charge is vital for mutual trust between vestry and committee and will help the vestry lead the church during the transition and help the committee represent the church effectively with candidates. **Tool 2** is a sample vestry charge to a search committee.

Some vestries form a separate committee to lead the congregation's reflection on where it is and where it is going and to produce a parish profile that the search committee can use to market the parish to prospective rectors. This is sometimes called a self-study committee. If a separate committee leads the vestry's and congregation's self-assessment and development of a parish profile, it is critical that the search committee absorb the results because their early interactions with candidates are the first step in forming a partnership with the next rector.

Bishop and Diocese

Your bishop will be your most important counselor in the rector transition, so engage him or her as soon as you know you are in a transition. I hope he or she knows your parish well and will have valuable insights. Be sensitive that it is hard for a bishop to know every church well because of broad duties, finite working hours, considerable travel time, and the tendency of problem situations to crowd out the time available for

---

[13] Geitz, *Calling Clergy,* 10.

healthy churches. Use the transition as an opportunity to help the bishop know your church more deeply and prepare to support you and your new rector in the future.

I refer to working with the bishop, but the bishop may delegate most direct contact with churches in transition to a "diocesan transition minister." This role often is part of the responsibilities of the canon to the ordinary. In addition to coaching lay leaders, transition ministers often maintain relationships with their counterparts in other dioceses, which can be helpful in identifying candidates.

Diocesan transition ministers have varied views on how to achieve successful transitions. The majority of diocesan transition ministers responding to a survey by Interim Ministries in The Episcopal Church were not trained in interim ministry. Surprisingly, when helping congregations find an interim rector, 31 percent of respondents preferred word-of-mouth to more structured sources.[14]

Many dioceses have unwritten lore about the bishop's preferences for transitions. For example, "He likes long transitions," or "She likes fast transitions." I suspect this lore usually extrapolates from limited data points. Your bishop knows better than we lay people that one size does not fit all. You need to understand the premises for the bishop's specific advice for your church.

Ignore the lore and ask good questions to benefit from his or her judgment, such as

- What are your specific dreams for our unique church?
- What do you see in our church today that affects the characteristics we should seek in our next rector?
- Looking at churches you shepherd that are most thriving, what observations could be relevant to our transition?
- Reflecting on the most successful rector transitions you have supported, what are lessons we can use in our transition? How should we plan to use stages of our transition, from concluding our outgoing rector's time with us through the interim period and the early months of beginning the partnership with our next rector?

The canons of The Episcopal Church (many dioceses also have related canons) describe the bishop's main formal task in a rector call, which is to indicate to your vestry that he or she is "satisfied" with your call of a new rector. This does not mean you must call the bishop's first choice, since the bishop is your counselor but not a participant in your

---

[14] "IMEC Survey," *IMEC Online Website*, http://imec-online.org.

discernment. The formal requirement is that the bishop will confirm satisfaction that your new rector is a "duly qualified Priest" who accepts the position as your rector.[15]

Your bishop understands deeply that this transition is a pivotal moment for your church. He or she is aiming for a strong pastoral relationship with your next rector at the same time as you are aiming for a ministry partnership with the rector. If by chance your bishop should disagree with any of the advice in this handbook, I hope the book will help you to ask better questions and make your discussions with him or her more complete. You and your bishop share the goal of a thriving, growing church and a congregation fully engaged in ministry.

The Episcopal Church

The Office for Transition Ministry of The Episcopal Church, or OTM, oversees resources for clergy deployment.[16] In addition to offering online reading about transitions and facilitating networking among diocesan transition ministers, the OTM operates a database of Clergy Ministry Portfolios, containing information that clergy provide about themselves and Ministry Portfolios provided by parishes and other institutions with open positions. Clergy may access the OTM system to see the Ministry Portfolios. Lay leaders are not authorized to use the database to see Clergy Ministry Portfolios, although your diocesan transition minister can review those on your behalf and you can ask candidates to send you their Portfolios directly. The OTM documents are discussed in later sections.

The transition ministry officers of the forty dioceses operate the Transition Ministry Conference, which augments the OTM system for those dioceses and holds periodic

---

[15] *Episcopal Church Canons*, c. III.9.3. (a)(3).

[16] The OTM is led by a priest experienced in parish transitions and guided by a 12-person board. According to Canon III.16. the Presiding Bishop appoints four bishops to the board, the President of the House of Deputies appoints four lay persons and four deacons or presbyters, and the General Convention confirms the appointments, under Canon III.16. In recent years some of the lay slots have been filled by clergy. In 2009 the OTM became the successor to the church's Clergy Deployment Office. A few people still refer to "CDO." If you hear or read "CDO," think OTM. Its resources currently are at www.episcopalchurch.org/page/transition-ministry and http://archive.episcopalchurch.org/transition/109541_21176_ENG_HTM.htm.

meetings of member dioceses.[17] The Conference's dioceses represent 47 percent of the total average Sunday attendance of the domestic dioceses. The Conference has a website where their churches may list open positions in a simpler format than the OTM's, and where clergy may register their openness to new calls, in a database seen only by diocesan officers with login rights.[18]

Interim Rector

Many churches need to engage an interim rector for pastoral care and continuity of worship services unless the interim period is expected to be quite brief. Also, if your church needs to deal with issues such as conflict over an issue facing the congregation, relationship stresses, or grief over losing a longtime rector, an interim rector with special skills can help you address those challenges and move toward a vibrant future.

Many interim rectors have retired as rectors and feel called to use their wisdom to serve congregations facing particular challenges. If you seek an interim rector, it makes sense to consider several and find one who fits your church and situation well.

There is not an obvious way to find interim rectors. Most seem to be identified by word of mouth, and you can ask for names of prospective interim rectors from your bishop, your former clergy, and priests who have visited your church. Some bishops provide their parishes a list of interim rectors. If your bishop does this, take full advantage of his or her recommendations by discussing why the bishop thinks each might be an excellent fit for your parish at this time.

Confirm early that you and your bishop or diocesan transition minister have a common understanding about the interim rector's qualifications and his or her role and responsibilities in this particular transition period. Canonically, an interim rector can be responsible for liturgical matters with the senior warden formally responsible for most other matters, such as overseeing the staff, facilities, and many scheduling

---

[17] The Transition Ministry Conference dioceses are Bethlehem, Central New York, Central Pennsylvania, Chicago, Connecticut, Delaware, East Carolina, Eastern Michigan, Easton, Indianapolis, Long Island, Maine, Maryland, Massachusetts, Michigan, Milwaukee, Missouri, New Hampshire, New Jersey, New York, Newark, North Carolina, Northern Indiana, Northwestern Pennsylvania, Ohio, Pennsylvania, Pittsburgh, Rhode Island, Rochester, Southern Ohio, Southern Virginia, Southwestern Virginia, Vermont, Virginia, Washington, West Virginia, Western Massachusetts, Western Michigan, Western New York, and Western North Carolina.

[18] *Transition Ministry Conference*, www.transitionministryconference.org.

matters.[19] Alternatively, the bishop can appoint the interim rector as priest-in-charge with the full set of responsibilities that a rector has. [20]

The Episcopal Church does not have a comprehensive system for churches in transition to identify and communicate with prospective interim rectors. Interim Ministries in The Episcopal Church includes Episcopal clergy who approach interim roles as a vocation, and your bishop or diocesan transition minister may be in contact with one of the other independent transition ministry organizations that include Episcopal priests. You also can post your job opening with the Episcopal Digital Network on its broader list of open positions.

An interim rector fills a key pastoral role. The transition naturally arouses feelings of uncertainty in the congregation, and the interim must be a non-anxious presence with the personality to connect with many parishioners quickly, the wisdom and intellect to preach and teach at a high level, the energy to meet unpredictable needs of the congregation, and the experience to understand and lead or support all the ministries of the church.

The interim rector generally should not be eligible to be a candidate for rector, nor should he or she participate in the discernment to call a new rector. An interim rector can assist with transition tasks not related to the candidates and discernment, such as helping the congregation update a sense of its identity and developing a profile to share with prospective candidates. The role of interim rector requires a high level of judgment about what *not* to do and about how to support the lay leadership as they step up to bigger roles in the transition.

 The vestry should enter into a formal letter of agreement with the interim rector regarding mutual expectations, compensation, amount of notice to be provided at the

---

[19] *ECC*, c.III.9.3.(b). Your diocese may have its own canons addressing transitions in more detail.

[20] I have heard of bishops giving a parish a short list of interim rector candidates and expecting that they would select only from that list, but I assume it is much more common for a bishop to consider all interim rector candidates who might fit the parish and whose calendar fits the transition timing. Moreover, a bishop almost always would welcome proactive lay leadership. Section III.9.3 of the Canons of The Episcopal Church, which applies to the appointment of rectors, also governs the appointment of interim rectors. It is silent about the process to be used to select an interim rector who fits.

end of the interim period, and other considerations.[21] Some of the section "Start Your Partnership with the New Rector" also applies to the start of an interim rectorship.

Search Consultant

After you read this handbook and begin to plan your transition, you should have a sense of whether you want to use a paid rector search consultant to assist with some of the process steps. There are a handful of individual consultants experienced in Episcopal rector searches. As of this writing, there appears to be no church-wide list of all consultants, but your diocesan leaders may know several and be able to tell you about their qualifications and recent successes that are relevant to your church.

A consultant can assist and be a sounding board on all steps of a transition. These tasks are not hard for lay leaders to master, but it can be helpful to have the support of someone who has been through other searches and to share the workload with an experienced hand. A consultant is not a matchmaker, nor can he or she discern God's call for your church. However, he or she can share process experience from other parish's searches and could be an experienced facilitator of discernment discussions. Consultants know a lot of priests and may be able to suggest a few prospective candidates to you. Remember, however, that if they know confidential information from other searches in which they have been involved, ethics may preclude them from giving you relevant information about the prospects.

If you use a consultant, be sure to agree clearly in writing about the tasks on which you do and don't want support. It is hard to manage the timeline of a rector search with its various participants and their unrelated calendars and with the need for secrecy. Discuss your general timeline with the consultant, and agree on expectations about deadlines and responsiveness.

Chaplain

Some committees enlist a chaplain who leads regular devotionals and prayer but does not participate in the confidential aspects of the search and discernment, while other committees save this spiritual leadership role to share among themselves. Our committee invited different parishioners to open every other meeting by leading a devotional. They did not stay for the confidential working meetings, but the time

---

[21] More advice on formal agreements can be found in Richard L. Ullman's paper, "Called to Work Together," available at the OTM website.

together strengthened our bond with the congregation. When we did not open our meetings with these devotionals we shared the Eucharist in a private service.

Rector Candidates

The discernment is mutual. Your search committee and the candidates independently and together are listening for God's call for your church and for their vocations. This means your candidates are the most important participants in your transition even though only the search committee will meet them or even know their names.

You will learn much from your candidates' questions about your church and their ideas for ministry and through your efforts to provide them an appreciation for your church. Above all, you will be inspired by their lives and ministries. Many people report this as the most rewarding aspect of their service on a search committee.

Manage the Ending Stage

How you and your outgoing rector manage his or her departure can set the stage for the success of your partnership with your next rector.[22] Ideally, when your vestry learns your church is in a transition it will not be a complete surprise because lay leaders and the rector have had candid annual discussions about succession. Seek the advice of your bishop then agree with the outgoing rector about exactly when his or her tenure will end. Make the most of his or her remaining time. Coordinate with the rector to ensure that communications are clear and consistent to prevent distracting rumors in the church.

Recognize the feeling of loss many of the congregation will feel upon losing a rector. This is the person with whom they have shared important times including personal crises, who has affected their spiritual journeys, who has invited and inspired them to ministry, who has been part of their lives. The depth of feeling can be significant. The longer the rector's tenure has been, the more parishioners are likely to be dealing with deep feelings of loss. You may need to provide a forum for people to acknowledge such feelings.

---

[22] At least two books focus on how critical the outgoing senior pastor's role is for the success of the next senior pastor: *Next: Pastoral Succession That Works*, by the Rev. William Vanderbloemen and Warren Bird and *Pastoral Transitions: From Endings to New Beginnings*, by Wm. Bud Phillips.

Recognize the sense of loss the rector feels upon leaving a congregation as well. In most cases he or she is being drawn to a new calling but nonetheless will feel a sense of loss and maybe some doubts. It is normal for a priest to feel regrets and to need time to let go of the period of ministry that is ending.

Oswald's *Running Through the Thistles: Terminating a Ministerial Relationship with a Parish* offers practical advice for clergy about how to leave a church and gives the lay reader a sense of what a departing priest may feel. The title refers to Oswald's childhood experience of running home from school barefoot, regularly crossing a Saskatchewan thistle field, and collapsing on the other side to pull briars out of his feet.[23] He wrote that the way to minimize the pain was to run fast over the narrowest part of the field and warned that for a priest to depart a church too fast would risk leaving with the briars of unresolved emotions.

The Ending Stage offers you an opportunity to set a tone of gratitude about the past and hopefulness for the future. Do not let the recent period just trail off; mark it consciously by honoring your outgoing rector and your life together. A celebratory and Spirit-filled conclusion of the period that is ending will help lead to the next period being Spirit-filled.

How to celebrate depends on your church's traditions. Your celebration may include parties, sharing photographs on bulletin boards and your social media sites, and special outreach events; there are many possibilities. Celebrate with something permanent, for example, hanging a portrait of your outgoing rector or photos of an important church event. Episcopalians have a gift for partying, so I offer no advice on this. Do it your way and make it a celebration that encompasses the whole congregation.

As you enter the In-between Stage of your transition, be encouraged by Loren Mead's observation after counseling hundreds of churches, "The most creative moments in a church's life happen when the pastor isn't there."[24]

Practical Planning

Address the details of the outgoing rector's employment, such as accrued vacation days and the timing and logistics of vacating the rectory if you have one.

---

[23] Oswald, *Running Through the Thistles*, 2.

[24] Leadership Education, *Loren Mead: importance of local church.*

Ask the outgoing rector to make lists and files to capture "everything you wish someone had told you when you arrived." Some notes should be given to the senior warden and other lay leaders now, and others should be sealed for the next rector. The outgoing rector certainly should include pastoral notes for the next rector and the interim rector. For example, who in the congregation has a life-threatening illness or is dealing with a major life change? Different rectors participate differently in church finances, but if the outgoing rector has "donor files" in his or her head, these should be written for the next rector to consider in his or her own way.

Plan for continuity in routine activities. Ask the outgoing rector to review his or her weekly calendar with the senior warden. Most of the time goes to ecclesiastical responsibilities, such as pastoral visits and sermon preparation, but note the other tasks he or she has handled by default, perhaps regarding facilities, administration, and communications. Lay leaders may be able to temporarily assume some of the rector's responsibilities in other areas, such as outreach ministries. Your bishop may be able to share a checklist of steps to ensure continuity.

The outgoing rector will work with the bishop and associate clergy, if you have them, to ensure the worship service rota is set for a period after he or she leaves and to clarify who will be on call for pastoral emergencies. Parishioners' daily lives and spiritual journeys do not pause for a rector transition. Pay close attention to how pastoral care is coordinated, not just obvious things such as hospital visits and being accessible for parishioners with pastoral concerns, but less obvious parts of maintaining a pastoral culture. For example, how does the church mark the birth of a parishioner's out-of-town grandchild, and how does it invite parishioners to visit with a priest or a trained lay person such as a Stephen Minister during times of personal stress?

Be highly supportive of the staff during the interim period. Not only is their workload likely heightened, they probably feel great uncertainty about the church and the future of their roles. Designate one or more lay leaders to sit with staff members to understand their weekly calendars and what they have scheduled in the coming months.

Review the numbers that measure church activities, such as attendance at worship services and regular church events, so you can be attuned to such measurements through the interim.

The Episcopal Church Foundation's Vital Practices website offers more detailed practical advice regarding the outgoing rector's departure, including a checklist of subjects to consider before the rector leaves.[25]

While departing, many pastors try to minimize the impact and act as if everything is normal.[26] Do not be complacent. Agree explicitly on the projects the rector will complete before leaving and determine who will assume other projects. Be realistic. The outgoing rector is in a sense a lame duck and may lack emotional energy for every wrap-up task you and he or she identify. The hours previously given to thinking and daydreaming about projects in your church will begin to be claimed by projects in his or her next role. Once when I resigned from the CEO role of a company, before I told the board I was leaving, a confidant advised me, "List everything you need to complete before you go. Strike at least half of the list that will be unrealistic. Finish the rest, and go." This advice ignores pastoral relationships but otherwise may fit.

Communicate with the Congregation

BE JOYFUL. BE GRATEFUL. BE CALM.

Share your feelings through the tone of every communication in your newsletter, in conversations in the church halls, wherever. Whatever the ups and downs of your congregation's past experience, constantly remind the congregation that your transition is an opportunity to increase the ministries within the congregation.

The purposes of church communications are to

1. maintain trust and support of church stalwarts and engage parishioners on the fringe,
2. lead everyone to envision the church's future and be ambassadors for it,
3. increase confidence in the transition process and the future and limit anxiety and false rumors, and
4. help the whole congregation prepare for the change the transition will bring.

---

[25] The departure checklist for lay leaders is available at www.ecfvp.org/files/uploads/4b - Exit Checklist for Lay Leaders 800912.pdf.

[26] Sweetser and McKinney wrote about this and developed exercises to help clergy say good-bye. Sweetser and McKinney, *Changing Pastors.*

Organize Church Communications

Here is a checklist to get you started:

1. Write responses to frequently asked questions (FAQs) you expect to receive. This helps the search committee to be confident and to speak with a shared voice.
2. Plan church listening sessions devoted to the transition. Have search committee members visit regular meetings of church organizations to answer questions about the transition. Face-to-face discussions will be vital in engaging the congregation in the transition. Since our church is large, we held more than twenty such discussions at the church and in homes, and all felt useful.
3. Discuss the transition on the church website and social media pages. Ideally, use a separate tab on your website or a separate site linked to it. You need not refresh the content as frequently as content on a news or ecommerce site, but do keep it up to date.
4. Provide updates in every church newsletter or comparable form of communication in the church and on whatever physical bulletin boards or digital displays your church uses. At first glance, this may seem daunting, but it usually takes less than half an hour to write a few paragraphs on common questions or a subject that may arise in a church listening session.

Communications can feel repetitive to the vestry and search committee, who are living the transition 24/7, but repetition is necessary in order to reach more of the congregation.

Keep your candidates in mind as you craft website communications. A portion of your congregation and most of your staff will read your written communications, but eventually 100 percent of your candidates will read every word carefully.

Tool 3 is a frequently asked questions worksheet.

Congregational Listening Sessions

Congregational discussions are important for the parishioners who attend the sessions and for others who will appreciate that the process is open to all. Here are some suggestions:

1. List former vestry members and other church leaders, and explicitly invite them to listening sessions.
2. Circulate a sign-in sheet at each session for names, contact information, and special comments.

3. Consider displaying graphics. These reinforce key points about the church and can be good conversation starters.

4. Start the sessions by introducing vestry and search committee members.

5. Provide an update on the transition and then take questions.

6. Use the FAQ responses you have written in addition to answering questions asked in the sessions.

7. Listen with a posture of yes, not no. For example, if a question feels negative, respond with optimism and openness; "That is fascinating, but it is not my experience; tell me more." This is valuable in the halls as well as in scheduled discussions.

8. Designate a committee member to take simple notes.

9. Expect that questions in the early meetings typically focus on the transition process. In later meetings you likely will hear more about parishioners' hopes and expectations for the church and can engage the congregation in the transition as addressed in the next two sections.

Most important, let everyone see in your face your faithful confidence about the transition. Your demeanor is more important than your words.

Assess the Church and Imagine Your Future

Will Rogers said, "It isn't what we don't know that gives us trouble, it's what we know that ain't so." This applies to how we understand our churches, our own church, and each other in church.

Our knowledge and memory of the past is incomplete and possibly incorrect. We often project personal experience where it doesn't fit, starting with our assumptions about why all of us are connected with the church. For example, some are drawn by the music, others by youth programs, and still others by outreach ministries. To lead a transition, lay leaders need a thoughtful, shared understanding of the church.

You also need to share a vision of your future. Much of the published advice on church transitions emphasizes understanding what the church is now and how everyone feels. A rector transition does stir memories, uncertainty about the future, and concern about pastoral needs, particularly if your transition is due to a traumatic event.

But you are aiming your transition at what your church can be, so invest as much energy in imagining the future as you do in understanding the past and sharing feelings about the present. Paul's letters to the early churches contain plenty of pastoral notes, but they are packed with instructions to *go* and *do* and *be*.

Before you begin thinking about your church, you might revisit the New Testament epistles, written to the flawed, fractious, loving, and courageous people of the early churches. They faced greater challenges and longer odds than any of today's churches, yet look at how they spread the word of Jesus Christ. The books on pastoral transitions quote various sections of the epistles, and different passages are on target for different churches and situations. Read and notice which passages may guide and inspire your church now.

The vestry, the search committee, and other lay leaders of the rector transition need to begin sharing an understanding of where the church has been and where it is going, and, then a little later, to engage the whole congregation in this thinking.

Understand Where You Are

Listen to each other carefully and aim for shared understanding. Often we remember the church's halcyon days without realizing that each of us has a different memory. Each of us is drawn by a unique set of relationships and memories. We project our own experiences and feelings onto others everywhere in life, but I think we may do it more in church, because our church connection usually is deeper than our connections with and through the other institutions in our lives.

Aim to understand what is distinctive or unique about your church. What are the core expressions of your congregation, the first descriptions that come to mind when you tell someone about it? It may be easy to observe how your church is different from other Christian churches in your town. It will enhance discussions with your rector candidates if you consider how you may differ from other Episcopal churches.

It might help to read Diana Butler Bass' *Christianity for the Rest of Us: How the Neighborhood Church Is Transforming the Faith*. She studied fifty mainline churches and developed in-depth case studies of how ten churches, including four Episcopal churches, model "signposts of renewal." The ten signposts are hospitality, discernment, healing, contemplation, testimony, diversity, justice, worship, reflection, and beauty.

My church values the fact that we have always held diverse viewpoints in community through all the social and political turmoil since our founding in 1945. One of our distinctive strengths is that we support each other and appreciate our differences as we seek personal and community understanding on difficult questions. We refer to ourselves as a "big tent" and relish that we are one of the largest "conservative"

Episcopal congregations, one of the largest "progressive" congregations, and one of the largest congregations of people who believe next week's outreach event is much more important than whatever else we could debate.

In these qualities our church is a paradigm of the Anglican Communion and The Episcopal Church. Anglicanism was born in political controversy and has for 500 years wrestled with theological discernment and political disagreements, all the while enriching both our members' spiritual lives and historic public debates across the world.

As you talk with fellow lay leaders, contact former rectors and associate clergy to ask for their thoughts on how you can use the transition most successfully to advance the ministries of the church. They are well aware of your transition and already praying for you. Our committee interviewed all our former rectors and interim rectors as well as several former associate rectors. Their insights and support were invaluable. We asked the former rectors to describe the church they expected on the day they joined us versus how they understood the church a year after they arrived. Our follow-up question was obvious: "How could the mutual discernment process with the search committee have given you a better understanding when you started?" These conversations prepared us for more thoughtful discernment conversations with candidates.

The natural place to start is with the congregation's stories about the recent past with your outgoing rector. You need to process your feelings and put these years in the longer context so you can plan without reactiveness. A search committee veteran in our church jokes about "the windshield wiper effect" of seeking the opposite of the last rector. In any case, it is essential to understand the rector-church partnerships in your recent past. Congregations typically define eras by rectors' tenures and are opinionated and even emotional about them, so start here to understand where you are.

Think about your history. It has shaped the congregation more than you realize. What communal memories are important? What are the reasons certain former clergy and lay leaders are remembered fondly?

If the parish has come to have a new identity over the past several years, considering the recent and older history will help you recognize this development. A related issue affects many parishes. The neighborhood or city around them may have changed more than they have, and their old sense of where they fit no longer applies.

As you understand and assess your church, take care not to apply frameworks that do not fit. Those of us who spend many hours in other institutions are susceptible to misusing conscious or subconscious ideas of how organizations work. A church is not like a business or law firm or hospital.

Congregations often are understood based on their size. Much of this thinking originated in congregational development work by the Rev. Arlin J. Rothauge on the staff of The Episcopal Church in the 1980s. His writings are referred to across mainline Protestant denominations. Rothauge distinguished among Family Churches with up to 50 regular worshipers, Pastoral Churches with 50 to 150 average Sunday worship attendance, Program Churches with 150 to 450 average attendance, and Resource Churches with over 450 average attendance.[27]

Do not let theories about congregational size confine how you think about your congregation. For a variety of reasons, such as changes in families, social media, and weekend travel habits, average worship attendance is a less adequate church descriptor than it may have been several decades ago. In his book aimed at lay leaders, *A Generous Community: Being the Church in a New Missionary Age*, the Rt. Rev. Andy Doyle, Bishop of Texas, calls the categorization of churches by size "our Procrustean bed." He appreciates the research into church sizes but wrote, "Today in the Diocese of Texas we say when you see one congregation, you see one congregation."[28]

Church Growth

Regardless of your congregation's size, one of your main goals is to grow in membership, engagement, and vitality, in accordance with the Great Commission: "And Jesus came and said to them, 'All authority in heaven and on earth has been given to me. Go therefore and make disciples of all nations, baptizing them in the name of the Father and of the Son and of the Holy Spirit, and teaching them to obey everything that I have commanded you. And remember, I am with you always, to the end of the age.'"[29]

---

[27] Alban at Duke Divinity School offers a short paper entitled "Building Blocks: An Anthropological Approach to Congregational Size" which contains a good contemporary summary of church size theory.

[28] Doyle, *Generous Community*, 59-60.

[29] Matthew 28:18-20.

You and the congregation will welcome your next rector's fresh ideas and other changes. Pursuit of growth, however, may bring some changes you will not like. Growth could mean, for example, that coffee hour feels different, or nametags become necessary to help newcomers connect in the congregation. Steps to make worship services more accessible or to facilitate larger attendance could require adapting your traditions. For example, some small congregations exchange the peace exuberantly until everyone has greeted everyone, which at some size becomes impractical.

If your church is already large, or you want to grow to hundreds of engaged members, you can gain insights from works by the late Rev. Lyle Schaller, a highly regarded church consultant who worked with hundreds of Episcopal churches. He wrote that large churches were more fragile in key ways, and he identified twenty-four distinct ways that large churches are different from smaller ones.[30] In particular Schaller notes that the larger the congregation,

- the greater the responsibility placed on the leadership to initiate ideas and work,
- "the more necessary it is to plan for the care of the members rather than assume it will happen spontaneously,"
- "the more important it is to have a carefully designed, systematic, and highly redundant internal communication system,"
- the more important it is to recognize and accept "... the senior minister cannot be *the* shepherd, or pastor, to *every* member, "
- the more complex the requirements of the staff, and
- "the greater the need for carefully disciplined planning and preparation of every event and program."

Schaller argued that larger churches do not have staffing economies to scale and that they actually need more staff in proportion to membership. He observed that many churches are staffed for decline rather than growth. Are you confident your church is staffed for growth? The answer could be less in the staff count than in the specific tasks on which each staff member is working.

Imagine Your Future

In addition to reflecting on history, imagine what your church can look like in the future. Most of us feel the church is out of date in various ways. In *A Generous Community: Being the Church in a New Missionary Age*, Doyle offered entertaining and

---

[30] Schaller, *Multiple Staff,* 17-26.

thought-provoking views of what ails us as well as some ways forward. He addressed churches of all sizes and called on lay leaders to bring our best efforts to the church as we do to our families and professional lives. Here is his vision for "Church Next," which I hope makes you curious to read the whole book:

- The future church will be driven by the Holy Spirit and co-created by God's people.
- It will build digital and real commons with a goal of collaboration at every level.
- It will seek unity above all else, even above uniformity.
- It will invest in a life that embraces randomness and creativity, allowing for locally led ministry in a variety of diverse contexts.
- It will become comfortable with interchangeable parts and reusing old traditions in new ways.
- Its organizational structure will change.
- It will change its manner of using authority and engage a ministry of all of God's people.
- It will expect increased participation at every level.
- It will have clear values and be vision-oriented and vision-driven.
- It will be a diaspora, but it will not become an island of castaways.
- It will measure different things from the usual standards for success.
- Its leadership will be organic and contextual.
- It will take risks.

Doyle's book has discussion questions at the end of its chapters, making it particularly valuable to read in community.

As you imagine what all of this means for your church, be courageous in thinking about goals and how you can measure results. You will want to conduct a strategic assessment and planning process with your new rector, but asking a few action-oriented questions now could help clarify qualities your congregation seeks in that rector. **Tool 4** offers questions to start church assessment discussions. It focuses on facts and parishioners' opinions, not feelings. If the congregation has strong feelings to process, you will need discussions addressing different questions, and perhaps you will need to engage a professional facilitator.

However you structure the discussions among lay leaders and the congregation, always keep your goals in mind. Consider how this transition will help your church fulfill its potential during the next few decades. The next rector may not serve for twenty years, but his or her influence will extend for that long. He or she will baptize babies, guide the Christian formation programs for children, marry adults, and pastor all ages through life transitions and surprises.

Engage the Congregation in the Transition

The next step is to engage the whole congregation in reflecting on the church's history, its strengths, and its potential. This will allow for group understanding and catharsis, if needed, through discussing past problems and present challenges. With the whole congregation and in early small group discussions, listen carefully to others' memories and dreams. No two of us has the exact same memory of the "good old days."

Most congregations have a few anxious members who are quick to recall the problems. You need to be honest about the negatives but guide the group to appreciate fully the positives as well. You may have shortcomings to work around, but your future will be built on your strengths. Celebrating the past and present with intention can influence the congregation to see everything in appropriate perspective and to renew their belief in the strengths.

It is a bigger, longer task to engage a larger congregation, and a more difficult task for ones that have had particular struggles in recent years. Your transition leaders need a consensus about the state of the church as preparation for discernment about the next rector, and it will raise the trajectory of the church if the congregation "owns" the understanding.

A healthy small church may need only a few intensive discussions with little intervening time to digest them in order to engage the congregation in supporting the transition. Geitz suggests thoughtful formats for structured discussions in her book, *Calling Clergy: A Spiritual and Practical Guide Through the Search Process.*

It is helpful for a cross-section of parishioners to answer simple questions such as "Why do I belong to this church?" "When has our church meant the most to me?" "How do I describe us to others?" and "How do non-members in our community describe us?"

From the beginning of your transition, lay leaders and the whole congregation will talk in hallway conversations and elsewhere about change they hope the rector transition will bring. It is easy to forget that the change we want will bring some change we will not like. In most churches it is worthwhile to have organized discussions about change and to include broad groups of parishioners. Throughout the transition, remind each other to maintain open minds and hearts about both the welcome changes and the uncomfortable ones.

Parish Survey

Many churches that have more members than can meet in one group discussion use written surveys in order to engage everyone. A survey provides useful data and anecdotes and helps engage the congregation in the transition process. It can help obtain input from people beyond "the regulars" who are most likely to participate in church listening sessions. Survey results can provide useful data and quotes for the parish profile you may develop later as the primary marketing document of your search.

If some among your congregation are upset about aspects of the recent past, the survey, particularly with its comment fields, will enable them to articulate and process their feelings. Whatever the good and bad of your immediate or more distant past, the survey can ask questions that encourage parishioners to envision the church's future and their roles in it.

A survey creates a powerful expectation that respondents will receive the results, so the survey is not completed until the results have been discussed satisfactorily. Schedule church discussions where you share results after the survey is closed. These may be the most energetic and insightful congregational discussions of your transition. Allow adequate time after closing your survey to evaluate the results. If you have many comment fields, you will be surprised how many hours it will take to absorb the comments.

Building a survey is a skill that calls for previous experience or careful study of the subject. It is beyond the scope of this book to make you a survey expert, but be aware of these points:

- High quality survey results depend on how the questions are stated and the survey's overall construction.
- Make the survey anonymous to increase the response rate and possibly improve the quality of responses, but allow for respondents to provide their names if they choose. Several of our parish's survey respondents asked for a follow-up conversation with a search committee member or a pastoral call from a priest.
- Market the survey strenuously. Use all of your channels for communication. Allow enough time to get responses. Communicate clearly the date the survey will close. Aim for a response count at least equal to your typical worship attendance.

- If you have parishioners who are uncomfortable with an online survey, offer it on paper as well. Arrange for an independent person to enter their responses confidentially into the digital system to be included in the analysis.
- Adding comment fields to some of your quantitative questions may capture good insights.
- Use the survey to encourage the congregation to expand their thinking about your ministries, rector transition, and future. The early conversations among the vestry and search committee may have raised subjects you can introduce to the whole congregation by asking about them in the survey.
- Survey results can help your next rector understand the church and guide the vestry and rector in decisions over the next couple of years.
- Make every question count. Longer surveys and longer questions mean fewer responses. This advice seems inconsistent with the preceding points, but you will find the balance that is right for your church.
- Include words that set a tone, including your church transition prayer, in the instructions at the beginning of the survey.

There are several online survey systems. The market leader, SurveyMonkey, is easy to use to create online surveys and to generate reports on the results. The free version allows ten questions and one hundred respondents and the "Standard" subscription, currently costing $37 per month, should be adequate to almost any church's needs. Alternatively, you can hire a consultant to conduct your survey.[31]

Tool 5 is a worksheet to start ideas for survey questions.

Timeline

From the moment you know you are in a rector transition a question on everyone's minds is, "How long will this take?" The question should be, "How long will it take to transition to the best possible result?" The answer depends on various factors.

---

[31] One firm, Holy Cow Consulting, has done over 950 church surveys over the past decade, including hundreds for Episcopal parishes. Holy Cow offers instant expertise and well proven surveys. Using their standard questions enables them to benchmark your results with other parishes.

Shorter Transition	Longer Transition
Healthy, happy congregational and pastoral relationships	Conflict, grief, or other issues
Previous rector's tenure was happy but shorter	Longer tenure with deep personal relationships
Church or location is attractive to candidates	Unattractive to many
Smaller, simpler church	Larger or more complex
Complacent congregation	Goal-oriented laity aiming for a dynamic future

A thriving small church may be able to complete a successful transition within a year from when the previous rector announces his or her departure until the next rector is up to speed and the new partnership is fully effective. In more complex situations, the preparation and discernment often take more than a year, and the integration of the new rector takes at least a year. We might like faster transitions, but the steps in a thoughtful transition simply take time, regardless of church size, to achieve the goal of a dynamic church with the laity and the next rector in a strong ministry partnership. The desire to rush reminds me of the old English proverb, "Marry in haste, repent at leisure."

Search committees typically begin their heaviest work when the outgoing rector leaves, because the interim period provides the opportunity for the lay leaders and congregation to reflect on the church's past and plan for its future. A few churches may be able to do much of this work effectively before the outgoing rector leaves if the church is quite healthy and the outgoing rector avoids any involvement. As you read the following sections, you may identify tasks your search committee and vestry can pursue effectively during the early phase of your transition.

The calendar and the liturgical seasons affect the search. Scheduling committee meetings is harder in July than October due to vacations and often more difficult during Holy Week and around Christmas. These limitations are relatively insignificant if you plan for them. Some search tasks call for work that can be done remotely using digital technology and others demand quiet study and contemplation outside of committee meetings. On the candidates' side, a priest who is in discernment with you may not be able to stop thinking about you and may write or speak with you anytime. Our committee was surprised that several candidates and prospective candidates contacted us during the days immediately before Christmas.

Regardless of your unique factors, good planning will help you progress steadily and enable you to adapt to the inevitable surprises that arise. I hope this handbook will help you determine the tasks you need to complete in each stage of your transition. **Tool 22** is a simplified project management worksheet to help develop your timeline by entering tentative deadlines for starting and completing tasks.

Transition Finances

In the midst of a big change, many of us focus on resource constraints. God's economy is based on abundance, not on limited resources that we must allocate. By all means, manage church funds carefully through the transition, but understand that your spending on this transition is an investment in the future of your church. Find a way to make the transition your church deserves.

Budget separately for the investment in the transition-specific costs for better planning and fewer financial surprises in overall church finances. **Tool 6** offers a sample budget. Be ready for "sticker shock." A small church transition might cost only a few thousand dollars, especially if the candidates are in the region. A large church transition that includes a national search, cross-country moving expenses, and many start-up activities for the new rector may cost over $100,000. The Diocese of California, which has a mix of about eighty mid-size and small churches, has looked at rector transition costs in recent years and expects a typical rector transition to cost a mid-size church about $50,000 in addition to a church's usual annual operating expenses.[32]

The vestry and search committee should establish a policy regarding who may spend church funds for the transition and how spending will be authorized and approved. Search committee members should track travel and other expenses to be reimbursed from the transition fund, both for accurate cost management and to ensure they are not expected to bear all their out-of-pocket costs personally.

It is useful to establish a separate account or fund to keep the transition expenses entirely separate from the church operating budget. Some parishioners may want to

---

[32] McCaskill (Treasurer, Episcopal Diocese of California), interview with author, November 2016.

contribute to this effort in addition to their annual giving, and your church may have other assets that would be appropriate to contribute to the fund. When you establish the fund, decide what will happen with any excess money at the end of the transition. Our vestry provided that any unspent money left in the fund on the new rector's first anniversary would go into another fund that we have to help pay for long-term clergy housing.

Discourage search committee members from absorbing their out-of-pocket expenses. If some would like to contribute financially, accept their tax-deductible donations and require them to submit expense reports so you build a complete record of the costs of the transition. Some expenses are harder to track than others, such as the costs of fuel and tolls when driving candidates around town or childcare during meetings.[33] If your transition fund cash is handled by someone who is not on the committee, the reporting will need to be vague about certain expenses, for example, "$500 for plane ticket to visit candidate" rather than "$500 for round-trip flight to candidate in Spokane."

Apart from the one-time investment in the transition itself, the vestry should watch overall church finances closely. Total contributions to annual operations tend to dip during rector transitions, regardless of church size, so the vestry should be attentive to overall church finances to avoid financial distractions during your transition.

Prepare the Search Committee for Group Discernment

As the search committee focuses on planning to seek candidates, working with the vestry to assess the church's needs, and the characteristics of a rector who would fit, the committee's most important early task is to prepare for the spiritual discernment it will pursue later.

Come Together as a Search Committee

Worship together before your first committee meeting to set in your hearts that this work is different from any you have ever done. Your search committee will try to listen to God's will for your church on behalf of the whole congregation. The first time our committee met was to share a private Eucharist. Our church is large and our vestry had

---

[33] A downloadable tool for expense reporting is available on www.RectorTransitions.com.

called a diverse committee, so none of us had met everyone before that afternoon. That first hour together set our path for the next fifteen months until our new rector joined the church.

Plan to worship together regularly throughout the search, in private services or by sitting together in regular church services. If your vestry or a church prayer ministry group has not already developed a prayer for your transition, do this as the first work of the search committee. As described above, communal prayer will unite the committee and the church.

Make prayer and worship the first norm of your committee, how you begin and conclude every meeting, how you celebrate joyful moments and how you pause in stressful moments. You can start with a Bible study or devotional led by a committee member or another parishioner. You could begin or end with the appropriate Daily Devotions for the time of day[34] or by simply praying together the transition prayer you have chosen.

Your search committee's discernment requires a strong foundation of trust and spiritual support for each other. Even if you already know each other well, don't take for granted that you are prepared to begin spiritual discernment together. Here are practical ideas for building the foundation to work together in the Spirit:

- The single most valuable thing a search committee can do to prepare for group discernment is to go on an all-day or overnight retreat as early as possible.
  - o Try to enlist a professional facilitator who understands rector transitions and group discernment.
  - o Discuss the individual gifts you bring to the process. Think less about your respective knowledge and experience regarding the church and more about who you are as people of faith.
- Have a relaxed discussion about your feelings as you begin the transition. Each member can comment on questions such as
  - o Why do I call our church home?
  - o What do I dream for our church?
  - o What frightens me about the search and transition?
  - o What stands out among all the advice we have received so far?

---

[34] See, for example, pages 137-139 of The Book of Common Prayer.

- Discuss 1 Corinthians 12, where Paul wrote about spiritual gifts and needs for all the different parts of the body of Christ.[35]
    - The differences that each of you brings to the transition tasks are essential. If all the parts of the body were the same, there would be no body. Pauline theology places individual spiritual growth in the context of the community. After all, Jesus taught us to pray, "Our Father...," not "My Father...."
    - We should be in awe of the uniqueness of others. I like the imagery of former Presiding Bishop Frank Griswold, "We grow as we bump off each other's angularities."[36]
- Discuss the beautiful thanksgiving prayer for wisdom and power in Ephesians 1:15-23.[37] Ephesians addresses concerns of all congregations, not just the one at Ephesus, and it is a grand call to ministry that you and your next rector will answer together.
- Complete a psychological profile and share your individual results. We often understand each other subconsciously through mental models formed from individual experience, so using a common model can help structure a discussion. This exercise can help you appreciate each person's gifts and recognize your predilections so they don't get in the way later in the discernment process.

---

[35] 1 Corinthians 12:17-20 reads, "If the whole body were an eye, where would the hearing be? If the whole body were hearing, where would smell be? But as it is, God arranged the members in the body, each one of them, as he chose. If all were a single member, where would the body be? As it is, there are many members yet one body."

[36] The Right Reverend Frank T. Griswold (25th Presiding Bishop of The Episcopal Church), in discussion with author, September 2015.

[37] "I have heard of your faith in the Lord Jesus and your love toward all the saints, and for this reason I do not cease to give thanks for you as I remember you in my prayers. I pray that the God of our Lord Jesus Christ, the Father of glory, may give you a spirit of wisdom and revelation as your come to know him, so that, with the eyes of your heart enlightened, you may know what is the hope to which he has called you, what are the riches of his glorious inheritance among the saints, and what is the immeasurable greatness of his power for us who believe, according to the working of his great power. God put this power to work in Christ when he raised him from the dead and seated him at his right hand in the heavenly places, far above all rule and authority and power and dominion, and above every name that is named, not only in this age but also in the age to come. And he has put all things under his feet and has made him the head over all things for the church, which is his body, the fullness of him who fills all in all."

- Profile examples include the Myers-Briggs Type Indicator, the Clifton StrengthsFinder, several Spiritual Gifts Inventory tools, the DiSC personality assessment, Predictive Index, and others.
- Personality profiling systems have limitations. Most are not supported by data published in peer-reviewed journals. Clinical psychologists warn that such profiles are not scientific because they oversimplify personalities, and none of us has a single mode of behavior all the time and in all situations. But these tools can make you more sensitive to individual differences and the behaviors that are more typical for each of us, and a discussion of your respective profiles may prepare you to work together more effectively.
- Many consultants would sell you assessment reports and services. One simple inexpensive approach is to answer the questionnaire in David Keirsey's and Marilyn Bates' 1978 book, *Please Understand Me: Character & Temperament Types*, which would enable you to self-score your Myers-Briggs types and have a lively, enlightening discussion.[38] Many Episcopal clergy are familiar with Myers-Briggs, and a few of our candidates used its language in conversations with us.

Search Committee Norms

Agree on some norms in advance, for example

- Aim for consensus decisions about candidates. No member will get his or her way on every point, nor possibly even on the candidate who ultimately is called as rector, but together you will seek God's will for the church.
- Recognize that everyone contributes different perspectives and gifts. Each voice matters.
- Emphasize listening rather than speaking. Don't fill every empty space; allow for pauses to respond rather than simply react to each other.
- Challenge each other and debate comfortably inside meetings, but speak with one voice outside meetings.
- Decide in advance which decisions will be made as a full committee, for example, decisions about candidates. Some committees go so far as not to discuss candidates outside of committee meetings rather than risk missing the full benefit of the committee's diverse backgrounds and perspectives. Do not discuss a

---

[38] Keirsey and Bates, *Please Understand Me*, 5-10.

candidate as a group until everyone has had the opportunity to prepare for the discussion.

- Agree that every member will feel responsible for all of the finalists. Candidates will not have assigned advocates on the committee.
- Commit to each other that you will make this a top calendar priority until the discernment is completed, even if this means rescheduling travel or deferring other responsibilities.
- Share the workload equitably. Delegate tasks so that it is clear who is responsible for each one, but in ways that do not exclude others' opinions about how a task is performed.
- Allow any member to call a timeout for prayer at any point in a meeting. In our committee's early months no one called timeout in a meeting, but in the closing months of intense discernment discussions those prayer breaks were essential.

Practical matters

- Scheduling a large committee of busy people is hard. Set your calendar with frequent meetings for several months ahead so members can schedule travel and other things around it. If you later find that some previously scheduled meetings are not needed, no one will complain when you cancel them.
- For setting additional meetings, you can use free online polling such as www.doodle.com.
- For setting assignments, for example who will take minutes or who will bring refreshments, you can use free services such as www.SignUpGenius.com.
- Some committees engage an outside administrator or consultant whose only role is to maintain files and assist with communications. Widespread familiarity with email and word processing makes administrative tasks and communications easier than in past decades, but someone must contribute these hours.
- Circulate agendas in advance, not only listing subjects to be covered, but also noting why each is on the agenda. State the intended outcome of the discussion— to decide something or to share information that cannot be covered online.
- Circulate meeting minutes within two days following each meeting, so that the summary will be fresh and the minutes can be used to track assignments and pending issues. Some committees have one scribe throughout, while others rotate the role because few people can participate fully in intense discussions and simultaneously take excellent minutes.

In addition to making you more efficient, setting up effective processes accelerates group trust.

Establish Search Confidentiality

The most critical work of your transition will be the discernment with your rector candidates. The mutual transparency required for this discernment depends squarely on confidentiality.

Imagine sharing deep, personal matters with a group of strangers, knowing that even a minor accidental leak could have terrible long-term repercussions. It could be devastating to a rector candidate's relationship with his or her current congregation if it were revealed that he or she had answered a note or phone call from you, never mind having entered into serious discussions with you. A dialogue with you has huge implications for a prospective candidate's spouse and family. I am impressed that our priests allow themselves to be as vulnerable as our clergy deployment approach requires.

The majority of your search must be totally and absolutely confidential! It is permissible to tell the church generally what the committee is working on at the time, and you should involve everyone in your congregation in discussing shared dreams for the future. However, you must never under any circumstances risk anyone outside the committee learning who is, may become, or has been a candidate. Confidential matters must not be shared outside the search committee with other parishioners, committee members' spouses, or anyone else. The requirement for confidentiality extends indefinitely.

Secrecy is challenging for most of us. We believe in transparent leadership, and we do not like to be obscure with our friends. But confidentiality is the foundation of establishing trust with candidates. It makes mutual spiritual discernment possible. **Tool 7** provides practical advice on confidentiality.

Understand the Role of a Rector

Having assessed your church together, everyone on the committee will be up to date on all aspects of the church, including the things for which your rector is responsible.

At least someone will be knowledgeable about each ministry of the church and about practical matters such as staffing, finances, and facilities.

Everyone on the committee should be thinking about rector effectiveness in areas you have determined are important to your church, including the topics below.

Pastoral Care

You probably are able to recognize whether a priest seems appropriately "pastoral" in various settings, such as a hospital room, a meeting at the church office, a confessional situation, a funeral, and so forth, but the diversity of your committee should ensure a more comprehensive impression of your candidates' pastoral styles.

- What seems to motivate a candidate's pastoral behavior? Most priests' pastoral work is grounded in personal faith and compassion for others, but a few seem driven by a need to be needed.
- How does he or she manage pastoral care? Consider how pastoral care tasks are built into his or her calendar, how pastoral needs of the congregation are tracked, and, for larger churches, how pastoral tasks are shared among multiple clergy.
- Does he or she understand pastoral issues in a sophisticated way? For example, to counsel a parishioner on a job loss, it may help to understand non-church workplaces, or to counsel a cancer patient it may help to have an understanding of the basics of common therapies. The most interesting example may be in the area of mental health. The psychiatric and psychological understanding of many issues has changed significantly in less than twenty years, and most of us carry outmoded assumptions about subjects such as addictions, autism, and post-traumatic stress disorders.[39]
- What are his or her habits to maintain mental, physical, and spiritual well being? Few professions are as emotionally demanding as the role of a pastor, and a priest must practice self-care and maintain healthy family relationships in order to be an effective pastor to others.

---

[39] *Mental Health: A Guide for Faith Leaders*, published by the American Psychiatric Association Foundation, offers a high level summary of issues. LifeWay Research published a thought provoking report on a survey of 1,000 Protestant pastors, involving faith-based perspectives on mental health.

Preaching

Our congregation values strong preaching both as part of meaningful worship services and because it helps to attract new members. The sermon is a rector's single best opportunity to touch every person present, and that opportunity comes every Sunday. When we think of priests we appreciate, preaching is often the reason.

All of us know when a sermon comforts us, provokes us to action, or engages our minds. You have heard hundreds of sermons. Some fell flat and others affected you days and months after the Sunday worship service. Have you thought about why?

It makes sense to invest a few hours before your search to ensure you have a sophisticated appreciation for preaching. Our committee enlisted the Rev. Alyce M. McKenzie, Professor of Preaching and Worship and Director of the Center for Preaching Excellence at SMU's Perkins School of Theology, to tutor us. We also shared our notes from watching sermons on YouTube to learn from each other. The following thoughts won't make you a preacher or homiletics expert, but I hope they will deepen your sense of why some sermons work so well and will give you greater awareness of how the preachers crafted those sermons.

Unlike search committees of past decades, you may be able to experience candidates' preaching long before you meet them, as you find their sermon videos and podcasts online. This remote participation is not the same as being in a live congregation but is quite valuable if you are prepared to learn from it.

When you listen to or watch a sermon, expect to learn more than its content and the craft of the preacher. Our committee was particularly struck by the observation of our bishop, the Rt. Rev. George Sumner, that when you listen to four or five sermons from the same preacher, the person begins to come through as well as the messages of the sermons.[40]

A sermon includes the answers to three questions. What to preach? So what? Now what? Anglicans have the gift of the lectionary that takes us through the whole Bible in a three year-cycle, so Episcopal sermons typically are based on the week's scripture readings (*What to preach?*) and lead the listeners to engage personally (*So what?*) and reach compelling conclusions (*Now what?*) that are relevant to their lives.

Answering the three questions well makes a sermon meaningful for any listener, but it particularly fits the expectations of Episcopalians. The notion of our famous three-

---

[40] Sumner (7th Bishop, Diocese of Dallas) interview by author, July 2015.

legged stool of scripture, tradition, and reason is vivid in our minds. We expect, maybe even subconsciously, that a sermon will give us a thoughtful and possibly new understanding of the scripture and will connect the Word with our own lives in ways we understand through both experience and logic so that we are moved to action.[41]

Sermon preparation typically begins with studying the text and concludes with planning the delivery. The focus of a sermon is its "claim," which aims to engage listeners at the deepest personal level. For a preacher to find his or her voice, he or she must develop a way to generate a sermonic claim week after week. Bishop Sumner says he studies the scripture early in the week and notices what aspects of the passages gnaw at him this time, and that insight leads him to the claim of his Sunday sermon.[42]

A sermon is aimed at a specific audience or congregation. Our committee watched YouTube videos of the renowned Episcopal preacher the Rev. Barbara Brown Taylor and noticed how she connected with congregations in Georgia and New York by using specific images and references that fit the location.

A sermon's claim must apply to the lives of the listeners. It draws on the scripture, engages their emotions, and calls them to a specific action or understanding. It should be possible to state the claim in one sentence.

Following are some observations on what makes a sermon effective:

- Intellectual structure. This structure often begins with a thoughtful exegesis of the text and educated decisions about what substance to include and what to exclude. Structure requires not only determining the claim, but also a coherent form so listeners don't leave saying, "Interesting, but I just didn't follow him today."

---

[41] The Episcopal Church website section titled "Sources of Authority" contains an excellent brief explanation of the three-legged stool. "The threefold sources of authority in Anglicanism are scripture, tradition, and reason. These three sources uphold and critique each other in a dynamic way. Scripture is the normative source for God's revelation and the source for all Christian teaching and reflection. Tradition passes down from generation to generation the church's ongoing experience of God's presence and activity. Reason is understood to include the human capacity to discern the truth in both rational and intuitive ways. It is not limited to logic as such. It takes into account and includes experience. Each of the three sources of authority must be perceived and interpreted in light of the other two."

[42] Sumner, interview.

- A fast start. We live with TV commercials that grab our attention and call us to action in fifteen seconds. A contemporary listener asks, "So what?" as the preacher steps to the pulpit. A sermon is a sprint. It must grab our interest in the first sentence and reach full stride in seconds.[43]

- A hook that catches our attention and prepares us for the rest of the sermon. There are many types of hooks, for example, sketching an interesting character, jumping into the middle of a story, stating an interesting generality, pointing out a conflict, or asking a provocative question. Our news media regularly use conflict as a hook, for example, reporting on personal aspects of political candidates' competition as well as the substance of their positions and abilities. The Methodist pastor the Rev. Sondra Willobee notes the old Irish proverb, "If you want someone's attention, start a fight."[44] Questions can be superb hooks, and Jesus used them brilliantly. "Who do you say that I am?" "Why did you doubt me?" "Which one was the neighbor?"[45]

- Vivid language and concrete details. Think of how Jesus yanked listeners into a different perspective. "The kingdom of God." "Consider the lilies of the field." "You are the salt of the earth." The prophets used imagery, plays on words, parables, and proverbs to get hearers' attention. Jesus used aphorisms, riddles, hyperbole, and parables.[46]

- Emotional delivery. If it is worth saying, it is worth saying with passion, enthusiasm, and conviction. This delivery needs to be authentic, not manipulative, so the emotions of the preacher can inspire an emotional response from the congregation. A compelling delivery is unlikely if the preacher must read the sermon.

- Do not omit the "Now what?" question, even if it may give offense. The late Rev. Peter Gomes, former Pusey Minister of Harvard University's Memorial Chapel, said it is difficult to preach the gospel as Jesus did without giving offense, and the world is full of people capable of being offended.[47]

---

[43] McMickle, *Shaping the Claim,* 38.

[44] Willobee, *The Write Stuff,* 13.

[45] Willobee, 20.

[46] Willobee, 91.

[47] McMickle, 70.

- Concision. A sermon should exclude any element that does not advance the claim.
- A strong finish. Professor McKenzie says, "Stick the landing," and teaches her students not to step into the pulpit without knowing the last line verbatim. She also advises them to stop as soon as the sermon is complete. She says, "Have you heard a preacher who made a good point but then was like a driver who keeps passing perfectly good freeway exits instead of getting off the road?"[48]
- Finally, the congregation should leave a worship service having heard not just a sermon, but the Word of God.

McKenzie and her colleague Professor John Holbert explore the preceding points in an engaging book, *What Not to Say*, which I wish every preacher would study.

Our committee refined our appreciation of preaching by using sermon listening sheets. **Tool 8** is my simplification of three formats that Professor McKenzie provided us.

Leadership

Every church, regardless of size, requires management of activities, processes, and volunteers. Many rectors must manage staff and have some understanding of church administration, and finances. Perhaps a rector could succeed with no managerial capability, but it would be a handicap. If you want your church to change meaningfully, your next rector needs leadership as well as management skills.

The words "leader" and "manager" evoke strong stereotypes and connotations in our society, and thousands of books describe these roles, often in overlapping terms. Your committee may not have complete agreement on what leaders and managers do, so it is worth a few minutes of discussion to ensure you are in sync on this.

The following are a few characteristics of a rector as a good manager:

- **Manages time well.** Knows where his or her time goes. Uses practical deadlines and understands the critical paths of projects, that is, the sequence and overlaps of steps toward a goal and how these determine the overall timeline.
- **Measures results.** Measuring church results is harder than keeping score in a ballgame or tracking sales in a shop, but there are relevant measures for almost every church activity, for example, number of participants in a ministry, number of non-parishioners at an event for the community, and amount contributed to an outreach mission. Members' spiritual health is hard to quantify, although one

---

[48]McKenzie, interview by author, November 2015.

seasoned priest suggested to me that even this has at least one quantitative proxy, which is increasing personal generosity.

- **Delegates effectively.** Delegation is a cycle of agreeing on mutual expectations for a task, then circling back at appropriate intervals to check the status of the work and update the expectations. A manager should neither abdicate responsibility nor micromanage, but rather should fit the discussion of expectations and the timing of status checks to the sophistication of the team and the complexity of the task.

- **Clearly defines decision-making roles.** Does not make every decision but ensures consensus on how both routine and one-time decisions are made.

- **Understands congregational systems.** Systems thinking means understanding both internal and external aspects of a church, such as membership, lay leaders, prospective members, financial resources, facilities, local community, and diocesan ties. A systems perspective requires a conceptual framework and an understanding of how all the pieces interrelate. Most Episcopal priests are familiar with Bowen Theory of Family Systems, developed by psychiatrist Dr. Murray Bowen. Most are familiar with a concept of a congregation as a family of families.[49]

- **Understands the roles of staff and volunteers.** Knows how the church's work gets done. Systematically helps staff develop their capabilities and improve their performance.

- **Puts processes in place wherever practical.** For example, a rector might train someone to prepare most of a monthly newsletter, based on standard content and formatting, rather than repeatedly creating the newsletter him- or herself.

- **Communicates.** Listens closely. Articulates what needs to be done and why.

- **Is organized.** Sets ambitious but realistic priorities. Takes good notes and keeps useful records.

- **Remains focused.** Tackles what needs to be done and is not deterred if it is painful, difficult, boring, or otherwise unpleasant.

---

[49] Many Episcopal priests have learned about family systems through *Generation to Generation: Family Process in Church and Synagogue*, by Rabbi Edwin Friedman. Another well-known book on congregational systems is *The Equipping Pastor: A Systems Approach to Congregational Leadership*, written by R. Paul Stevens and Phil Collins and originally published by The Alban Institute in 1993.

The following are some salient leadership characteristics:

- **Loves people and is a servant.** Many favorite characters of the Bible were servant leaders.
- **Is visionary.** Sees what is possible, and sees the best in us. It is not easy to identify vision in candidates at first, but as you get to know them you can explore what animates their ministries in general and what excites them about the possibility of a call to your church.
- **Knows him- or herself.** Fits his or her gifts to the role, and seeks help as needed. Think of how Moses called on Aaron to help him communicate.
- **Tells the truth.** Makes everyone face facts. Methodist Bishop William Willimon wrote an excellent article about this called, "Truth Telling in the Parish," arguing that the church depends on clergy who tell us things that are painful to hear.[50]

Leadership and management without noble goals are meaningless at best and destructive at worst. Your rector's leadership should be directed to helping your congregation be its best in the characteristics that make up your unique identity.

Summarize the Rector Characteristics You Seek

Who Is Eligible

You may call any ordained Episcopal priest in good standing or a priest in good standing in a Church in full communion with The Episcopal Church, which includes Anglican Churches in communion with the See of Canterbury, The Evangelical Lutheran Church in America, and a few others, according to Canon III. 10. 2. (a.) (3).[51] Priests must retire at age seventy-two but remain eligible for short-term roles, less

---

[50] *Christian Century*, "Why leaders are a pain."

[51] It is not common for parishes actively to seek a pastor from other denominations that are canonically accepted, but not unheard of for small Episcopal parishes to combine with or share a pastor with other denominations. If you would like to consider candidates outside The Episcopal Church, start conversations with your bishop and the other denomination's bishop in your area.

than twelve months but renewable under certain conditions, according to Canon III.9.8. Check your diocesan canons for any other requirements.

You should not accept your interim rector or a current associate rector as a candidate unless you intend not to seek other candidates. This advice is not in the church canons, but most bishops strongly advise against calling someone currently serving the church. A priest who already knows you well cannot bring fresh perceptions and objective ideas to the church. Also, no matter how wonderful the person already in your midst, calling him or her could risk dividing the church.

The presence of an internal candidate is not likely to remain secret, so there is a real risk of division during the interim period, which would continue after the call. Any rector will disenchant some parishioners for some reason someday, and the problems for the church could be greater if they feel he or she had an inside track to the position. Also, if external prospects perceive there is an internal candidate, they will be less likely to commit to discernment with you.

Be sure that you are open to nontraditional candidates. It is hard to imagine in 2018, but statistics suggest that in many places women priests are considered nontraditional rector candidates. The Episcopal Church Office for Transition Ministry has an excellent set of resources, aptly named "Cast Wide the Net," to help you give full consideration to women candidates.[52]

Who Is Available

Your church and your next rector will come together as the result of deep mutual spiritual discernment. When you begin to seek candidates, only God will know who could be your next rector. Many priests, however, may be interested to take the first step in discernment with a congregation whose potential is evidenced by their effort to complete an energetic, Spirit-filled rector transition.

The Episcopal Church has published demographic summaries of active clergy in the fifty states, excluding foreign countries and territories. The reports define active priests to include full-time, part-time, interim, and non-stipendiary priests but not emeritus, retired, or supply priests.[53]

---

[52] *The Episcopal Church*, "Cast Wide the Net," www.episcopalchurch.org/cast-wide-net.

[53] Supply priests serve on short-term assignments and are paid on an hourly rate.

As of 2015, these reports represent almost 7,300 priests, stratified by gender, title, and age:[54]

- Senior priest on a multi-priest staff: 414 women and 1,140 men.
- Solo priest: 1,314 women and 2,474 men.
- Curates and associates: 853 women and 1,084 men.

o Age under 45: 15.1 percent.
o Age 45 – 54: 17.5 percent.
o Age 55 – 64: 34.1 percent.
o Age 65 and older: 33.2 percent.

Recruitment in any profession should take into account the issues of dual-career marriages. Of particular interest, 14 percent of active priests are married to another Episcopal priest, which the OTM has noted as a challenge and an opportunity.[55]

Priests' personal qualities, experience, and capabilities are more important criteria than age, gender, marital situation, and current role. Consider also that fifty-five of the ninety-nine domestic dioceses have sixty or fewer active priests, only twenty-four dioceses have over one hundred active clergy, and only nine have over 150 active clergy. These statistics indicate that if you do not seek candidates from beyond your diocese, you may be fishing in too small a pond.

For The Episcopal Church as a body, the demographic data suggest the health of our parishes depends on intensive focus on clergy deployment. According to parochial reports filed for the year 2014, we had 6,553 parishes and about 7,271 active priests. These numbers do not consider the positions filled by priests in schools, seminaries, and other non-parish roles, nor how well the clergy and congregations fit each other geographically and otherwise. The fact that two-thirds of our active priests are fifty-five or older is an actuarial challenge for The Episcopal Church.[56] How you approach your unique transition is more important than these church-wide statistics.

---

[54] The totals for roles and ages differ by six priests, which is statistically insignificant and could reflect simply that the reports were created in different weeks. See Hadaway, *Priests by Diocese, Gender, and Position* and Hadaway, *Age Distribution*.

[55] OTM Board, "An Invitation to the Church," The Episcopal Church, https://extranet.generalconvention.org/staff/minutes/download?id=1865.

[56] "The State of the Clergy 2012" by the Church Pension Group's Office of Research goes further, addressing subjects such as geographic movement of clergy, ordination trends, and the effect of age at ordination on clergy career paths.

How Many Candidates Should You Have?

You will benefit from having at least several compelling candidates. Going through the mutual discernment process with multiple candidates in the same time period will make your discernment deeper and more effective, and you will see your church in new ways as you discuss it with multiple candidates. This deeper insight will better prepare you to build a partnership with your next rector. At the same time, the discussions with you can help all of your candidates in their personal discernment and in their relationships with their current and future congregations.

Characteristics of a Rector Who "Fits"

By now your committee has a consensus on the qualities you seek, ones that would be nice to have, and those you do not want. You may be reminded of the popular version of Supreme Court Justice Potter Stewart's quote regarding obscenity, "I can't define it, but I know it when I see it." Your discernment discussions, however, will be deep and wide, so it will help you to state your consensus now. No one will fit all your criteria perfectly. All rectors will need others around them to complement their gifts, and different rectors will need different types of support from the congregation. **Tool 9** is a worksheet to help you discuss rector criteria.

Develop Your Marketing Material

The church website is not only a compelling evangelism tool but is also the first place many prospective rector candidates may learn about the church. Be sure it is attractive and up-to-date.

Many Episcopal churches in transition introduce themselves to prospective candidates with a parish profile that describes the church, the city, a vision for the future, characteristics sought in a rector, and so forth. This profile serves multiple purposes:

- It distills the church's understanding of where it is and where it wants to go. The profile can encourage the church to dream and stretch.

- It markets to potential candidates and people who may be able to refer good candidates. It helps them to get past superficial or secondhand impressions to and to see the church's potential.

- It helps set up effective discernment dialogues between the committee and candidates by framing some of the subjects to discuss and by accelerating candidates' understanding of the church.

- It helps you introduce the city or town. Do not assume all of your candidates already know your area or that they understand why you love it; tell them.

- It enables you to share photographs, which can convey more meaning than anything you can write. Some churches even introduce themselves through a video and link to it from the profile.

- Your parish profile should appear on your website. It could be formatted like the rest of your web content, although now it is typical for a large Episcopal church to present its profile as an online flipbook that also is downloadable as a .pdf file. Be aware that formatting and writing that work well on a monitor may differ from what traditionally has been considered effective in print.

- It advertises what you seek in a rector and how prospective candidates should contact you.

Be sure to write in one voice. The primary author of our profile was a parishioner who is a journalism professor with skills ensuring our profile would work well both digitally and in print. Our committee provided initial content, and when we edited the drafts, our rule was that we should comment "in the margins" but leave the actual wording to our expert author.

It takes a lot of work to produce a parish profile and the audience is small. Thus, the hours invested may have a small return in the number of readers. One of the readers, however, will be your next rector and the energy and care reflected in the profile will speak to him or her. The profile will set the stage for later discussions with candidates. Our committee even produced a short video entitled, "We Are Praying for You." We did not expect to receive the most hits on YouTube, but we believed it would help bring us together with our next rector.

Tool 10a is a worksheet to prompt thoughts on how the profile covers your church's history, worship, Christian formation, pastoral care, outreach, fellowship, staffing, leadership, facilities, finances, diocese, city and region, parish survey results, and dreams for the future.

Material developed for your profile will help you list the job with the OTM, as discussed later. Keep those records you collect but decide not to include in the final version of your profile because they may be useful later. For example, the detailed information on church ministries may contribute to discussions with candidates and to subsequent planning with your new rector.

Introduction to Spiritual Discernment

In the opening paragraph of *An Introduction to Ministry*, Ian Markham and Oran Warder wrote, "We begin and end in the knowledge that we, all of us, are known and loved by God. We begin and end in the knowledge that God summons us into relationship, invites us to share in his divine life, and calls us to ministry in the world."[57]

What does it mean to be called by God? How do we hear the call? How do we know the call is from God and not one of the many other voices calling to us in our busy, loud culture? These questions reflect the essence of spiritual discernment.

None of us can master spiritual discernment in a lifetime. Most of us have few occasions to pursue a group consensus through spiritual discernment. We may pray for guidance many times, but how do we recognize God's guidance? To help prepare your search committee for its central task, this section introduces some of Christianity's wisdom about this topic.

Ignatius of Loyola

Studies of spiritual discernment often start with Saint Ignatius of Loyola, the Spanish priest who founded the Society of Jesus (the Jesuits). In 1548 Ignatius published *Spiritual Exercises*, a collection of prayers and other writings intended to guide a four-week retreat with the objective of determining one's life purpose. *Spiritual Exercises* included twenty-two "rules" for discernment – and has been an essential source for Christians, inspiring countless books, university courses, and church conferences for over 450 years.[58]

Among the countless publications on Ignatian discernment, *Weeds Among the Wheat: Discernment: Where Prayer and Action Meet* is an influential and relatively recent book. In it, the late Rev. Thomas H. Green, S.J., who taught theology at the Ateneo de Manila

---

[57] Markham and Warder, *Introduction to Ministry*, 7.

[58] One well-organized online resource that is accessible to any reader is www.IgnatianSpirituality.com, which is maintained by Loyola Press.

University, unpacked Ignatius and "the art and gift" of discernment for committed lay persons not trained in theology.

Understanding the meaning of discernment is necessary before we work on the mechanics of it. Green reviewed the role of discernment in the Old and New Testaments and the life of Jesus before exploring Ignatius's thinking. He argued that God is not a "watchmaker" who presets all of our actions, nor a puppeteer managing our actions. If God were either, our discernment would be meaningless. He analogized God as the father of adult children with free will and the maturity to discern without the need for explicit instructions in every situation. He urged us to apply rigorous independent thinking and argued that Ignatius thought that asking questions and making suggestions were "...an integral part of the discerning process of obedience..."[59]

Ignatius emphasized the necessity to discern. Green notes that Ignatius's first set of fourteen rules involve "...the time of beginnings – of conversion from a worldly or mediocre life, of honest self-confrontation before God." The next eight rules are about commitment, "...of putting on Christ, of filling our emptiness with the fullness of Jesus."[60] The book title refers to preparation and timing for discernment, coming from the parable of the sower, who, as weeds sprout amidst the wheat he had sown, must wait until the plants have grown enough so he can discern between wheat and weeds.[61]

Part I of the book, "Preparing the Soil," is a good metaphor for a search committee preparing for discernment. Green observed that the principles of discernment are not obscure, although establishing the *climate* of discernment" is extremely difficult. Green wrote, "It is my belief that a community will not find corporate discernment difficult *if* the individual members are prayerful, discerning persons, and that such communal discernment will be impossible if the members of the community are not persons of prayer and discernment."[62]

A weeklong conference of Jesuit scholars in 1968 discussed the applicability of Ignatius's works to modern times. It resulted in *Studies in the Spirituality of Jesuits: Ignatian Discernment*, a now classic paper by the late Rev. John Carroll Futrell, S.J.,

---

[59] Green, *Weeds Among the Wheat*, 39.

[60] Green, 105.

[61] Matthew 12:24-30.

[62] Green, 17.

written for American Jesuits and other Christian communities. It is relevant for every Episcopalian rector search committee. The paper observes that we live in a representative democracy with lobbyists and majority rule, and the ways we commonly experience consensus differ from the consensus that comes from spiritual discernment, which is not about balancing what different members of the group want, but about hearing God's call. Reflect on this thought early in your transition so it is second nature when you reach the last stage of discernment with your final candidates.

Spiritual discernment requires *feeling* God's call more than *thinking* our way to it. Green pointed out that Ignatius's second set of rules exclusively uses feeling words: "It is the feelings we discern and not the thoughts. There is perhaps no point about discernment which is so little realized or understood as this, especially in cultures and religious traditions where feelings are given little value or are considered suspect."[63] Futrell summarized what discernment feels like and warned it may surprise us. "Ignatian contentment is the profound peace experienced in recognizing that one has heard and responded to the word of God—a word which is often disconcerting and unexpected and a call to share in the Cross of Christ."[64]

Listening Hearts

In 1987 a powerful ministry was started at Memorial Episcopal Church in Baltimore by Suzanne Farnham, the wife of its then rector. The original objective involved using the model of a Quaker clearness committee to help individuals discover their vocations. A clearness committee gathers to help a member find clarity in a difficult issue and integrates wisdom from "other major strands of Christian spirituality – Benedictine, Carmelite, Ignatian, Anglican, Protestant, Orthodox, and Jungian."[65]

Forty people began Memorial Church's study by reading classic spiritual literature and interviewing Christian leaders. They pursued four threads: call, ministry, discernment, and community. They began writing a discernment program manual, which grew into a book, *Listening Hearts: Discerning Call in Community*. The resulting ministry provides workshops, retreats, and speakers and has produced several more books. Its website, http://listeninghearts.org/, is an excellent resource.

---

[63] Green, 98.

[64] Futrell, "Ignatian Discernment."

[65] "History," *Listening Hearts Ministry.*

Practicing Discernment

Listening Hearts describes conditions you can create to help discern God's call, including[66]

- Trust in God and one another.

- Commitment to listen with open hearts and minds, especially for what you do not want to hear.

- Prayer and total attentiveness to the presence of Christ.

- Knowledge of scripture, which is our access to the experience of God's people in history.

- Humility, which requires accepting the uniqueness of our individual experience and limited nature of our knowledge.

- Preparation. Farnham said, "...it is important that you do the best research you can, evaluate it, weigh it ... but..., 'that is only the preparation.'"[67]

- Discipline and perseverance, which require, among other things, setting aside the necessary time.

- Patience and urgency. Wait patiently, but don't dawdle.

- Perspective. Let discernment rest lightly; your priority is to know and love God.

The diversity of your group can improve the quality of your discernment *if* everyone can listen to each other. Sister McKinney noted that our culture is biased "...in favor of rational, linear thinkers and assertive verbal folks—and against folks who come to or express wisdom through hunch, intuition, silence, story, and arts."[68] You want the full insight of every member of your committee.

Listening Hearts provides practical advice in one particularly concise list.

---

[66] Farnham, *Listening Hearts*, 25-30.

[67] Stannard, "Spirit speaks to us."

[68] Olsen, "Delighted and Disillusioned."

Discernment Listening Guidelines from *Listening Hearts*[69]

The goal of spiritual discernment is to receive God's guidance.

1. Take time to become settled in God's presence.

2. Listen to others with your entire self (senses, feelings, intuition, imagination, and rational faculties).

3. Do not interrupt.

4. Pause between speakers to absorb what has been said.

5. Do not formulate what you want to say while someone else is speaking.

6. Speak for yourself only, expressing your own thoughts and feelings, referring to your own experiences. Avoid being hypothetical. Steer away from broad generalizations.

7. Do not challenge what others say.

8. Listen to the group as a whole—to those who have not spoken as well as to those who have.

9. Generally leave space for anyone who may want to speak a first time before speaking a second time.

10. Hold your desires and opinions — even your convictions — lightly.

Our committee studied Ignatian methodology together early in our transition and applied it throughout our discernment. The following table lays out the practical process that resulted and worked well for us.

---

[69] *Listening Hearts Ministry*, "Discernment Listening Guidelines."

A Practical Ignatian Process for a Search Committee

Sequence of Steps	Examples
Pray. Remind yourselves that you expect to hear God's call through each other's voices.	
Identify a clear yes or no question for discussion, and frame it as a positive statement.	"We should continue in discernment with ___name___." "We should call ___name___ as our next rector."
Go around the room with each person saying only one point against the statement, with a scribe writing each point on a flip chart. When everyone has spoken once, continue, with no one speaking a third time until everyone has been invited to speak twice. Continue in this way until no one has a new point for the list.	"We have services in both English and Spanish, and his Spanish skills are only rudimentary."
Set aside the negatives. Pray for inner freedom and ability to hear each other's voices.	
Repeat the circuit with everyone making single points in favor of the statement.	"She has successful experience with church schools."
Again, pray for inner freedom and ability to hear each other's voices.	

Sequence of Steps	Examples
List and review the positive and negative points. Notice as a group that not all points are of equal significance.	"He is a highly effective Bible teacher" is more significant than "Her motorcycle riding will seem odd in our community."
Review the negative points and distinguish between facts and fears. Some fears are questions to answer with more research. Some fears are actually risks that may be manageable.	"Our recent history of conflict calls for a lot of pastoral experience, and he has been ordained for less than one year." – Fact "I am not sure his Spanish language skills are adequate." – Question. "She has never lived in our state, and we do not know how she will adjust to it." – Manageable Risk.
Set the list aside and pray another time for inner freedom and ability to hear each other's voices.	
Have each person share his or her thoughts at this stage.	

Save your lists of points from each meeting until your last discernment meeting in case a member wants to refer to a previous discussion or finds it helpful to see consensus emerging over several discussions.

You will feel tired at times in your discussions, and you likely will have moments when one or more members are frustrated or emotional. Break for a while and then start back with a communal prayer. Stress may arise from diverse members having different communication and decision-making styles, and the committee chair(s) must keep everyone focused toward the same end.

Do not expect a unanimous consensus. Consider your personal points about a candidate and whether you feel some point so strongly that you would disagree if most of the committee's consensus were on the other side. In the language of Quaker discernment, would you "stand against" the group consensus, or would you make your point but "stand aside?" Either could be the right position.

A consensus about a candidate may develop organically without many hours of discussion. More likely, over a few scheduled discussions, you may move slowly from a sense of confusion over your own and each other's feelings and toward a shared sense of the candidate and a common vision of how he or she could fit with your church.

I promise two things about this methodical process. First, it is counter to our prevailing culture and will feel frustratingly slow to some of your members. Second, it will give you the opportunity to hear God through every member, so that together you discern God's call for the church.

What Will God's Call Feel Like?

As we seek consensus, how can we recognize a call is from God? Based on the sources reviewed above, some signs of God's call *may* include

- Joy.
- A sudden sense of clarity.
- A temporary experience of disorientation, followed by calm and serenity.
- Tears that are comforting and tranquilizing.
- Strands of experience that seem unrelated begin to converge together.
- Persistence. The message keeps recurring through different channels.
- Peace, which is the central sign. This peace is not the same as the absence of trouble, but a firm conviction that *the Lord is risen* and "all shall be well."[70]

Ultimately, your discernment may feel somewhat messy. In the words of Presbyterian minister and author, the Rev. Chuck Olsen, "Somehow God is not going to let us rest with the assurance that we have some kind of iron-clad formula for discerning

---

[70] Adapted from *Listening Hearts,* "Signs of the Spirit."

decisions. That is not always the way the Spirit works. The mystery remains and infiltrates all of our best human efforts."[71]

If the discernment task seems daunting, you will appreciate Suzanne Farnham's words in an interview for *Episcopal Life Magazine*. "If you notice, in Scripture, time and time again God calls people to do things for which they do not have the gifts, or at least the apparent gifts," says Farnham. "God often calls us to do things that we do not have the ability to do. Spiritual discernment is, if God calls you to do something, God empowers you to do it."[72]

The Listening Hearts website may be the most efficient group discernment resource at your fingertips. Green's book on Ignatian discernment is readable and engaging, but if 200 pages are more than you want to tackle now, Christian counselor and writer David Sandel has a good, concise summary of the book on his blog site.[73] The other sources I refer to are listed at the end of the handbook. Our committee enjoyed studying during our transition, but I gained more from some of the material mentioned here after we called our new rector. Our committee's discernment had felt mysterious as we reached its conclusion, and the subsequent study helped me make a little more sense of the experience.

Although group discernment may seem unfamiliar, we have every reason to approach it with confidence. "I will instruct you and teach you the way you should go; I will counsel you with my eye upon you."[74]

---

[71] This quote is from a fascinating two page article on group discernment on the website of Alban at Duke Divinity School. It was written by the Rev. Charles M. (Chuck) Olsen, a retired Presbyterian pastor and the founder of the Worshipful-Work: Center for Transforming Religious Leadership. Olsen has written widely on practices to bring spirituality into church leadership, including books on group discernment.

[72] Stannard, "Episcopal Life."

[73] Sandel, "Weeds Among the Wheat."

[74] Psalm 32:8.

"Cast the Net" – Find Candidates

Identify Prospective Candidates

Advertise your opening in whatever recruitment channels your diocese provides and by submitting a Ministry Portfolio to the OTM. The Ministry Portfolio calls for basic facts as well as answers to twelve questions about the church. The OTM will show your Ministry Portfolio in its database. Clergy can log in to the database to see open positions. **Tool 10b** is a worksheet to help you think about your inputs to the OTM's template.[75] **Tool 10c** is the worksheet for completing the Transition Ministry Conference's Open Positions Form that is used in forty dioceses.

Do not limit your marketing to the OTM database. Its detailed standard format cannot fit every church's situation and its database is closed to non-clergy, so your listing cannot be shared like a good marketing document can be, whether digital or in print. The Episcopal News Service posts parish openings on its public website[76] for the first two or three months after it receives them. It directs clergy to the closed OTM database to see positions that have been open longer.

Listing in the usual places will target priests who on some level have decided they are open to a new call, but your next rector could be a priest who has not considered leaving his or her current ministry. Simon Peter, Andrew, James, and John expected lifetime careers as fishermen on the Sea of Galilee until Jesus called them. Our broad search identified over 150 prospective candidates, and all but three were referred to us outside of the OTM listing system. I do not know whether this was typical, or whether some would have found us through the listing if we had not found them first, but it does demonstrate the importance of referrals.

Consider how you can use the web to advertise to the world and generate referrals from more sources. Share your parish profile with friends in other places, parishioners who have moved away, your bishop, your former clergy, recent guest preachers, and others. Most importantly, ask your entire congregation to tell the search committee about priests they have met or heard.

---

[75] Your diocesan transition minister may authorize a Search Chair to receive a password to be able to post your Ministry Portfolio, but this does not extend to reading clergy listings.

[76] "Job & Calls," *Episcopal News Service,*
https://www.episcopalnewsservice.org/jobs/?type=clergy

Our committee found it helpful to create a one-page prospect summary on each priest whose name we received. **Tool 11** shows an example. We found most of the information from public sources online, but some is available in the *Episcopal Clerical Directory*, which is revised every odd-numbered year by Church Pension Group. It took twenty to thirty minutes to complete each summary.[77]

Set up a list to keep track of prospective candidates throughout the process, as they become candidates and through the steps of mutual discernment. **Tool 12** is a worksheet you can adapt to track candidates.

Invite Prospects to Become Candidates

Have open hearts and minds as you cast the net for candidates. Our committee wrote every priest who was referred to us as a prospective candidate and invited each to take a step in discernment with us. Based on the prospect summaries alone a handful of prospects seemed unlikely based on geographic location, age, or some other reason, but we invited all of them. We could not know what God had in mind, and every name had been offered by someone who cared about our church. Ultimately, several of the most compelling candidates were priests who might have seemed unlikely based on our first, superficial impressions. **Tool 13a** is a sample letter inviting a priest into mutual discernment.

Typically a prospective candidate formally becomes a candidate when he or she updates the Clergy Ministry Portfolio on file with the OTM and submits it to the church conducting the search. Many committees require additional material. Our committee required a resume, which in many cases elicited information beyond the standard format of the Clergy Ministry Portfolio. We also asked for a cover letter discussing the candidate's possible fit with our church. The insight gained from these letters in many instances set the stage for subsequent mutually helpful conversations.

---

[77] The *Episcopal Clerical Directory* includes all living priests and lists diocese of canonical residence, current church and position and address (or home address if not now in parish ministry), current diocesan and church positions, birth year and parents' names, post-secondary degrees, years and schools, diaconate and ordination dates and bishop, wedding date and spouse's name, previous positions since ordination, including church or other institution and dates, published books, and some awards. The *Episcopal Clerical Directory* may seem antiquated in the age of LinkedIn and online directories, but it is helpful. A subset of the Episcopal Clerical Directory's information was posted online recently at www.ecdplus.org. Having an online directory is a positive development and will prove even more valuable as priests get into the habit of keeping their online profiles up to date.

You may have a subject specific to your church that you want to explore early in the mutual discernment. For example, perhaps you would like to know candidates' experience with a particular issue facing your local community or their ability to continue a particular initiative your church has underway.

Be clear about the material that will comprise a complete candidate file, and state the requirements where prospects will see them, such as in your parish profile, on your website, or with your diocesan transition minister. Establish procedures to list each priest who indicates the intention to be a candidate and to note when his or her file is complete. Be sure no candidate omits sending any of your required material. Our committee designated one person to determine when each file was complete and to advise the candidates that we had all the necessary material. **Tool 13b** is a sample email notifying a priest that the file is complete.

As priests become candidates, remember their perspective. Entering a search makes them vulnerable, not only with you but also with their families and in some sense with their churches. You are asking them to consider the time-consuming, hard work of a written and verbal dialogue with you and the deeper work of listening for a possible new vocational call. Be sensitive, personal, and extremely confidential. Be aware that on days you are not in contact with them, they will be thinking about you and wondering what is happening on your side of the discernment process. Pray for them.

You will be reminded that most clergy think of their vocational lives differently from most people in other professional roles. In his book, *A Passion for the Possible: A Message to U.S. Churches*, the late Presbyterian minister the Rev. William Sloane Coffin distinguished between a career and a calling in words that often are quoted in both church and secular settings.

> A career seeks to be successful, a calling to be valuable. A career tries to make money; a calling tries to make a difference... A career, we can say, demands technical intelligence to learn a skill, to find out how to get from here to there. A calling demands critical intelligence to question whether "there" is worth going toward... A calling sees service as the purpose of life... It is not against ambition, but considers ambition a good servant and a bad master.[78]

Establish a personal point of contact with each formal candidate and keep him or her apprised of what the committee is doing through every step. Because our search was

---

[78] Coffin, *Passion for the Possible*, 77.

large, we worried about being impersonal. Each of our committee members became the process "shepherd" for a few candidates. This was not to complicate our process but to ensure that every candidate had the personal phone number of a committee member and felt comfortable calling him or her for any reason. Even with this system, it was a challenge to personalize our large process.

Agree in advance how you will coordinate the discernment process with your bishop or diocesan transition minister. Many of them will want you to coordinate with them with communications processes they have established while supporting other parishes' successful transitions. Update them at regular intervals so they can be ready to serve as sounding boards at points when their input will help you.

In addition to praying for our church and our rector transition, our parish prayer for the transition mentioned priests in discernment. As we learned the names of candidates, this part of our prayer became more meaningful to us. It felt as if we were recognizing each of them as a special servant of God.

Finally, as your prospects become candidates, don't simply be reactive. You can reach out to encourage them to consider entering discernment with you. Our committee reviewed our prospect summaries and in many cases researched further by reading the websites of the prospects' churches, following web links to their social media pages, and watching or listening to their sermons online. We discussed our impressions and identified priests we particularly hoped would enter discernment with us. Many of these people did offer themselves as candidates, and we made personal phone calls to the others, asking them to pray about it and consider taking a first step with us. Several of these interactions involved two or three long conversations over a month or so; all were valuable for our search and personally rewarding for us, and the priests commented on how much they appreciated the conversations.

Initial Discernment

Reading and Research

Start files on each candidate, including the prospect summaries you made before the prospect became a candidate, their OTM Clergy Ministry Portfolios, and any other documents you have requested from them. The summaries' links to their church websites, sermons, and social media pages are valuable. Secure digital files are much more efficient than centrally stored paper files because they enable users to access the files from remote locations and click on web links while reading. Our committee subscribed to Dropbox for Business, which enabled strong security and worked well on the range of devices our members used.[79]

The OTM Clergy Ministry Portfolio, shown as **Tool 14b,** includes eleven essay questions. These questions are relevant to every church but may be incomplete for your church, because it is hard for one size to fit all. Many search committees ask candidates to answer a few questions in addition those in the OTM Clergy Ministry Portfolio. If a candidate obviously does not meet your basic requirements, respectfully tell them rather than send them additional written questions that would take hours to answer.

Any written questions you choose to ask will help candidates understand your church and will lead you into rich conversations with them through the rest of your discernment process. It may feel challenging to limit yourselves to seeking only a few written responses, but remember this is not your last opportunity to ask questions of candidates who continue in the discernment process. **Tool 14a** is a worksheet for written questions to help you consider what you should learn from your candidates before talking with them.

During our committee's preparation for discernment, we became convinced the number one thing we wanted to discuss with candidates was their personal faith. The OTM's Clergy Ministry Portfolio does not address this, so our first supplemental question was "Please discuss your call to ministry and your daily walk with Jesus Christ."

Keep Notes on Candidates

As you get to know your rector candidates, first from reading about them and later from meeting them, you will find it is challenging to remember all your impressions. It is also hard to distinguish among your preliminary impressions, firmly formed opinions, and aspects about which you have partially formed opinions due to having only partial information.

---

[79] The online files took a few days to set up and required members who already used Dropbox to establish new accounts under different email addresses.

The downloadable version of **Tool 9** is formatted to help you clarify rector qualities you are seeking and to capture impressions to help you form opinions. Each committee member can adapt this form to make personal notes to bring to the group discernment discussions. No one needs detailed notes or good penmanship. The point is to jot a few words to remind each member of points to share for group discernment.

These simple notes will help every committee member think more clearly about the candidates, by encouraging more comprehensive impressions. Psychologists have proven that we make many decisions with intuition while believing we decided by rational deliberation.[80] Groups can reach more robust judgments than individuals, but this depends on each person bringing independent input to the group's discussion.[81] It will be valuable to keep simple notes when you read candidate files, and when you interview and meet them.

Early Discernment Decisions

The first big moment of discernment is deciding which candidates to interview. Have all committee members study the written files on each prospect and listen to a sermon or two, then meet to discuss your impressions. Be sure the entire committee is present. Start with a worship service or devotional that centers everyone.

Until this point you will have allowed yourselves to be open to all candidates who have entered your process. You will respect and like all of them and will appreciate how they have shared themselves with you. It will be hard emotionally to conclude that some of them do not fit your church's needs and should not continue in the process.

As you discuss the candidates, make notes where everyone can see them on a flip chart, which is better than a whiteboard because it can be reviewed at subsequent meetings. You may want to organize your notes by rector qualities or by pros and cons.

If your committee has a strong, shared sense that you want to continue to the next step of your process with a candidate or a clear sense you do not feel called to continue with a particular candidate, recognize your consensus and focus discussion where you are still seeking consensus.

---

[80] Among numerous recent books about how we think, versus how we think we think, one of the best is *Thinking, Fast and Slow*, by Daniel Kahneman, whose work in behavioral psychology won the Nobel Prize in Economics.

[81] Kahneman, 82-85.

Many search committees in discernment with more than a handful of candidates use a color-coded scheme to create a visual image of their consensus. Consider the following approach:

1. List each candidate on a wall chart.
2. Give each committee member green, yellow, and red sticky dots from an office supply store.
3. Ask each member to place a green dot near the name of each candidate with whom they want to continue in discernment, a red dot near the name of each candidate whom they feel should not continue, and a yellow dot near the name of any candidate about whom they are open-minded.
4. It will become obvious where you have consensus and which candidates need more discussion.
5. Allow significant time to discuss candidates with all green dots. Even when committee members agree on a candidate whom everyone hopes will continue in the process, your reasons will differ and you should identify your questions about them.

When you schedule interviews, be sure to make warm contact with the candidates you don't intend to interview further. Tell them why you appreciate and are impressed with them, but clearly say you do not feel called to continue in discernment with them. Some candidates may ask for detailed explanations, or ask, "What could I have done differently?" In these moments, as I do in my business career, I say that I prefer not to have a detailed discussion when I am delivering the news, but that I would be available to talk in a few days. That subsequent conversation is less likely to be emotional, and the candidate and I will be more likely to listen to each other well.

Interviewing

An interview should be your next contact with those candidates who seem to fit best. Standard interviews with clichéd questions and answers can be uninformative for both parties. Your objective is to avoid triteness and formality, and to have a structure that helps you and your candidates with discernment. Ask useful questions in a good setting that is conducive to making a deep connection.

We sometimes form strong opinions based on brief first impressions, which is problematic when judging something as complex and multi-faceted as a candidate's potential fit as your rector.[82] The roles of a rector are not narrowly specific and few members of a search committee deeply understand all of them or all of the relevant characteristics of a church. The advice below will help you go deeper than your first impressions.

Interview Advice

- First, absorb what you can from written material and online sources. This research makes interviews and structured conversations an opportunity to validate what you have learned from reading and to allow you new and deeper insights.

- Aim to relax a candidate with your initial questions, thereby reducing the risk of both parties presenting themselves in a pro forma way rather than beginning a real dialogue.

- Ask a candidate's story from the beginning, not in the reverse chronological order of most resumes. You want to understand their formative experiences and the choices that have defined their path. You cannot practically probe a candidate's toddler years, but childhood matters. Most of the social-emotional development and over 90 percent of the biological development of the brain occurs before kindergarten.

- Explore their experience, and ask second, third and fourth level questions. For example, "Why did you decide to do it that way?" "What surprised you as the situation unfolded?" "How did you adapt?" "What alternatives did you consider?" "How did others react when you did 'x' or when 'y' happened?" "In retrospect, what were the key factors that led to the ultimate outcome?"

- Sometimes you do not need to be specific. Merely ask them to tell you more.

- In digging into the candidates' important experiences, put them in the context of their paths, and notice how they learned and grew in judgment and capabilities. How do you imagine them adapting to fit with your church today and its potential over the next several years?

- Pay attention to what drew them to the priesthood and what motivates them vocationally now. Since The Episcopal Church is so distinguished by our liturgy

---

[82] A major theme of Kahneman's *Thinking, Fast and Slow* is that all of us frequently make decisions based on fast, flawed inputs and all the while we believe that we are weighing valid inputs logically.

and many of us feel it so deeply, you may want to probe your candidates' liturgical preferences. Today it seems many priests describe their preferences as "broad church," but this vague term calls for deeper exploration.

- Avoid hypothetical questions. Do not ask, "How would you handle 'x'?" Ask instead, "Tell me about a time when you did 'x'." This will allow a deeper and more objective discussion and will help you to avoid projecting qualities onto a candidate.

- Listen much more than talk. Don't fill the empty spaces; let the candidate do that.

- Listen below the surface. Do you hear what you expect? What traits appear in the answers? What validates or contradicts your previous thoughts? Where does the candidate tend to go deeper or not to go deep? Notice what is omitted as well as what is said.

- Listen for self-image, dreams and motivations, regrets and concerns, bitterness and joy.

- Don't hesitate to ask deep questions in a first interview. First conversations can be especially illuminating since they occur before both parties know the other well enough to say things they know, even unconsciously, that the other wants to hear.

- Use the discussion to explore how the candidate's experience and capabilities fit your church's needs. Candidates tend to be in one of three categories. For some, there is abundant evidence that they fit well. Others demonstrate strong potential to become good fits. And some others clearly do not fit well and appear unlikely to become good fits.

You need not ask every question in one interview; you can always call a candidate and ask additional or follow-up questions later.

To understand how a candidate fits with the rector criteria you have developed, list your subjects in advance with sample questions you can use to open each subject. **Tool 14c** is a worksheet for planning interviews, which adds to the written question worksheet of **Tool 14a** as it provides examples of questions that may be more useful to guide a conversation rather than eliciting written responses. The downloadable version combines both sets of questions.

It probably will help your discernment to use the same interview set-up with each candidate. For those who are distant, you can have videoconferences. Since so much of personal communication is visual, with facial expressions and body language, you should take advantage of pervasive, easy-to-use video technology.

Videoconferences require more work to set up well than do one-on-one video calls on a phone. You can use FaceTime, Skype, or another videoconferencing service. Set up a computer with a camera and large monitor in a room with good acoustics and no background distractions. Depending on your set-up and camera quality, you should be able to have up to four committee members visible on a candidate's screen. More than four is too many for a fluid conversation with a candidate and, with typical camera set-ups, their faces might be too small for the candidate to read their expressions. Other committee members can sit off-camera. You can improve the quality of the images your candidates see, and see them closer to life-size, by using a little more equipment, such as a peripheral camera, and throwing a candidate's image onto a large television monitor, or by using more advanced videoconferencing equipment.

Tell each candidate in advance how long the interview will last, and include time for the candidate to ask questions. Our committee provided the first question in advance, which seemed to help make the interviews comfortable and informative. We prepared some questions that we asked of all candidates and we also asked each of them one or more questions that we tailored to his or her particular background and interests.

For each interview, designate a team captain whose role it is to introduce the committee members, both on- and off-camera, and to manage the flow of discussion. Plan your questions and decide in advance who will ask each question. To allow the members on-camera to focus intently on the discussion, leave the video equipment and the clock monitoring to those participants who are off-camera.

Record the interviews so committee members who cannot attend can watch them later. Simple software currently available for this includes Pamela for Skype and Apowersoft Mac Screen Recorder for FaceTime. A digital file setup on Dropbox for Business can hold over a dozen one-hour videos without the cost of an upgrade to additional storage.

As soon as possible after your first set of interviews, set an unrushed meeting for your whole committee to discuss the candidates. Start the meeting with worship or a centering exercise. Remind everyone of the discernment discussion approach you have decided to use, perhaps drawing on the Listening Hearts and Ignatian summaries above. It may be useful to bring out your green, yellow, and red dots again and to tape to the wall your notes from previous discussions of these candidates.

Be comfortable with blunt comments, trusting your confidentiality and the relationships you have built. None of your candidates is perfect or a perfect fit for your church. The impressions you form from reading a file and a video interview will be incomplete, but you need to share them as preparation for meeting candidates in person.

Since you now will be discussing real people, not abstract characteristics on a job description, you may find yourselves circling back to your rector specifications and weighting your criteria, or you may alter them based on what you have learned from talking with the actual candidates. Refer to the parish profile, the survey if you did one, and the early discussions of what the church needs now.

I predict that at some moment someone will say, "I wish we could combine the _____ qualities of Candidate A with the _____ of Candidate B." This is a positive sign that you have multiple strong candidates and that your discussions are getting deeper.

When you have reached prayerful conclusions, contact all of the candidates by phone. Begin to schedule personal visits with the ones with whom you feel called to further discernment. Tell the others you value them but do not feel called to further discernment with them.

There is no right number of finalists. You need multiple finalists because you should expect that, after meeting personally, some will not feel called to your church or you may feel some do not fit as well as you had expected.

Concluding Discernment

The next step is to meet your final candidates in person. You can send a small team to visit each candidate and his or her church, a visit that should include participating in Sunday worship services. You may host the candidates and their spouses in your town. Only a few committee members should visit a candidate, due to the risk of parishioners recognizing that their priest is in discernment with another church. Our committee now confidentially enjoys funny stories about our visiting teams' efforts to keep visits confidential. In some instances, members pretended to be married or to be parent and child, and once members scrambled to avoid being seen by a fellow parishioner in a distant airport.

Traditionally, a search committee tended to initiate personal contact with a candidate by sending a small team to visit the candidate, followed by the candidate's visit to the search committee. The downside to this approach is that it placed great weight on the judgment of the team making the visit. Now more churches are choosing to host candidate visits before traveling to visit them or even forgoing visits to candidates' current churches. This development may reflect that churches are less homogeneous than several decades ago, so they feel the need for the diversity and wisdom of the full committee in the first personal meetings with candidates. It may reflect that the full committee has seen the candidates online and possibly "met" them through videoconferences. Financial considerations may also play a role, as it usually costs less to host a visit from two people than to send three or four out of town. Regardless of the motivating factors, this approach has the advantage of allowing the candidate to interact with more people and, therefore, to develop a broader perspective of the congregation.

Visits from Candidates

Visits from each final candidate could include

- Worshipping together, perhaps in a Home Communion with the candidate as celebrant.
- Several small group conversations with the candidate and his or her spouse for every committee member.
- Tours of your church's facilities and your town for the candidate and spouse. Use members' expertise; some may be better guides for certain parts of the visit.
- A visit to your rectory if you have one.
- Time for questions you want to ask that did not fit into the video interview.
- A Bible study led by the candidate.
- A confidential briefing and small group discussion for the candidate on any particular issues facing the church.
- An interesting shared experience that prompts spontaneous conversation well outside the territory of interviews. Our committee got to know candidates differently in small groups walking in a park, visiting an art museum, touring residential neighborhoods, and visiting local facilities that interested the candidates.

Some churches ask candidates to preach for the search committee and possibly the vestry. This is off-putting to some candidates because it can feel more like an audition than part of a courtship. In the age of sermon videos and podcasts, it also may seem outdated.

Plan the visit to ensure confidentiality. Our committee hosted most of the meals in our homes and avoided public places where a parishioner might have seen us.

Some churches include the vestry in some aspects of the candidate's visits to the church. This is tricky because of the risk of adding people to the circle of confidentiality who have not built a powerful practice of confidentiality in the preceding months. In addition, it may be hard for some vestry members to understand that they must participate by contributing impressions to the search committee's discernment process rather than having "votes."

Visiting and meeting the committee is important for a married candidate's spouse. Depending on family, career, and personal considerations, the spouse may or may not intend to be active in the church, but he or she needs an opportunity to gain a good sense of the church. Likewise, the committee will understand the candidate better through exposure to his or her most important personal relationship.

Each committee member should take a few notes during the visit. How does the candidate react in different situations? What excites him or her, and what gives him or her pause? What is your gut feeling about how he or she would fit with the various members of your congregation? How does the candidate's spouse react? How do your interactions evolve through the visit? How can you imagine the candidate and spouse settling into your community?

An adequate visit takes at least a day and a night. I have heard several bishops describe the partnership between a rector and a congregation as a marriage. In light of this analogy, one overnight visit seems brief. It will take longer to introduce a candidate to a large church or a large city. Extend hospitality in the style of your church throughout the visit. For example, our committee prepared welcome baskets for the visitors and sent follow-up notes after the visits.

The hours are intense for the visitors, so be sure to schedule some down time when they can relax away from the committee. **Tool 15** is a sample schedule that you can adapt.

Visits to Candidates

Your visits to your final candidates provide an opportunity to experience their current churches and to sense how they are settled in their current communities. Experiencing a candidate's current church will not tell you what your church would be like with him or her as rector, but it can spark new conversations to get to know him or her more deeply.

Look for signs that a candidate is happy, settled, and successful in his or her current ministries. Try to observe how the staff and parishioners relate to him or her. How does he or she communicate with varied people and in different situations?

How do you experience the congregation and its worship service? What aspects of the experience can you attribute to your candidate rather than to the DNA of the church? You can share your impressions with candidate and ask questions, such as "How has the church changed during your years here?" "Why do you do _____ with this congregation?" and "What would you expect us to notice?" If you visit a candidate at a multi-clergy church, research the other clergy so that you and the candidate can discuss the roles of the other clergy and his or her relationships with them.

The visit to a candidate will help you understand better his or her current church's evangelism and outreach programs, as well as other aspects of his or her current ministry. You can gain a better perspective on what his or her current experience, and what he or she has learned from it, could mean for your church.

Some search committees do not visit any of their candidates at their current churches. Whatever your committee decides, be consistent; visit all or none of your final candidates. This consistency is vital to your discernment discussions and affects the candidates' perceptions of your fairness.

The visits to and from the candidates will yield intellectual and gut feelings for how the candidates match the rector criteria you developed earlier in the search. No one can be a perfect fit. Challenge yourselves to consider each candidate comprehensively. Continue to maintain open minds about who could be your next rector.

Candidate References

Get references from those people whom you expect to have different perspectives on your candidates, know them in different ways, and have been close to them at different times of their lives. Do not hesitate to ask for references beyond those listed in the candidate's OTM Clergy Ministry Profile. References from former supervisors, for example, rectors under whom a candidate served as an associate rector, are valuable if they are fairly recent.

Lay references are especially important. You are aiming for a strong ministry partnership with your new rector, so it is vital to have candid conversations with lay leaders who have had partnerships with your candidates. Their perspectives can give your lay search committee more to discuss than those you may obtain from the candidates' bishops, seminary professors, and ordained friends. Some search committees insist on a reference from a recent warden at a candidate's current church, and I have heard stories of these references containing key information not obtained anywhere else.

The OTM Clergy Ministry Profile requests six clergy references and only two that could be either clergy or lay, but many priests do not list lay references there. In our large search I saw the OTM Profiles of scores of priests and was surprised and disappointed by how few offered lay references.

The reference interviews must be conducted by a search committee member. No one else would have the nuanced preparation derived from your discernment discussions. Our committee designated the same member to make all reference calls on a given candidate, listening for themes across the calls and gathering insights from one call to frame questions for the next.

Even though your candidates will have listed their references, ask their permission again before you make contacts; the candidates may want to talk with their references first. Note that while it can be useful in business recruiting to ask a candidate's references to suggest additional references, this practice is uncommon in clergy recruiting and could upset your candidates.

Tool 16 offers ideas for the discussions with references.

Background Checks

Background checks are different from reference interviews. They involve an aspect of recruiting we would rather avoid because it makes us uncomfortable, namely the possibility that a candidate has a record of inappropriate behavior such as sexual or financial misconduct. You need to understand this step, however, and do it well.

A contemporary background check typically emphasizes safeguarding children and may include criminal history, credit and motor vehicle records, education credentials, and written reports from references provided by the candidates. In addition to reducing risks, conducting a background check can also help to protect your church and diocese against financial liabilities related to charges of misconduct. Your bishop will require a background report before deeming a candidate duly qualified. Screening reports on clergy are provided to bishops or diocesan transition ministers but not to lay leaders.

Your church may have a relationship with an employment screening company; if not, your diocese certainly does. Dioceses know which companies have proven their vigilance and efficiency in past screenings, and can be relied on for a background check involving a priest. Before you and the diocese decide which screener to use, understand its practices:

- Does its staff understand the best practices of safe churches and safe schools?
- How does it conduct criminal background checks? There is not a complete national database of criminal records, so a thorough check must review state and local records in candidates' past domiciles. Some jurisdictions' records are not searchable in a matter of minutes, but I am not aware of any that take more than a few days to respond to screening companies.
- Does it rely solely on written responses from references, or does it interview them by telephone?
- Does it check social media? This can be informative, but recognize that information obtained from social media generally cannot be used legally as the basis for not hiring a candidate.

Be sure to determine in advance how long the check will take. Some screening companies do not work with urgency, relying primarily on regular mail and accepting slow responses from references. If your diocese urges you to use a slow company, you can at least insist that the screening firm use email and have your candidates personally request their references to reply promptly.

Final Discernment

The last miles of discernment are exciting, as your committee feels energy about the approaching call, nervousness about possible news leaks, and urgency about coordinating the next steps of your transition. Be steady and stay close to each other, to your final candidates, and to your bishop or diocesan transition minister in these final days.

Do not be surprised to learn at this stage that some of your candidates are in discernment with other churches at the same time. It is possible that your first contact with these candidates occurred when they were beginning to feel they had accomplished what they could in their current roles and they were open to you and other churches. Also, once the family disruption of one possible move is on the table, it is not as big a step to begin considering other possible moves.

By this point, you will have developed a deep connection with your final candidates and will be able to have sensitive conversations about how the timeline of your discernment fits with their parallel processes of discernment with other churches. You can help them and your church by keeping up a good pace.

Regardless of the discernment approach you have chosen, whether from this handbook or other sources, you likely will feel a sense of mystery about how you reached this moment. Some committees have a fairly smooth path to consensus about God's call for their churches. Others feel they are walking across a rocky field. Sometimes it feels as if God removed a large stone to make a path, and sometimes it feels as if God placed a stone in the way to force a turn. Our committee's journey took many turns during the five months and scores of hours that we met after all our candidates were officially in the process. There were surprises, a few moments of anger in the room, a few tears, a lot of laughing, and ultimately a sense of mystery as God led us to a consensus.

Practical Aspects of the Call

At this point you and your new rector feel God calling you together. You are moving from discernment and your church's In-between Stage to setting up the partnership in ministry with your new rector. It will be joyful to share the moment of the call, and your attention to the details at this point is vital for completing the groundwork for your church's coming years.

Formal Requirements

Your committee might feel a circular logic in the formal call. You need to tell your new rector your committee feels God is leading you to call him or her, and you need to hear the candidate say, "Yes, I feel called to you." The formal call, however, is issued by the vestry, and according to Canon III.9.3.(a) of The Episcopal Church, you need your Ecclesiastical Authority, typically a bishop, to indicate within sixty days that he or she "...is satisfied that the person so elected is a duly qualified Priest and that such Priest has accepted the office to which elected…"[83] Moreover, your committee and your new rector should confirm conceptual agreement on certain points before you formalize the call. These points include timing, compensation, housing, and other practical considerations.

Here is a sequence that would serve the spiritual discernment and call process as outlined in this handbook:

1. Determine at the start of your search how many candidates your bishop would like to review personally. For some small churches the answer may be all of them; with a discernment process that begins with many candidates, however, he or she may prefer to review a smaller number during a later stage of discernment.

2. Help your bishop with his or her review. Your bishop may want to read your search committee's files on the agreed group of candidates and almost surely will want to meet your new rector personally before the call is finalized. Even if the bishop knows your potential rector, he or she will want to discuss this call with him or her. These meetings can be done during candidate visits to your church or on special trips for this purpose. Schedule the visit(s) at a discreet location away from the diocesan offices to protect confidentiality. Diocesan staff members are no better than others at keeping secrets.

3. Outline essential practical matters with your final candidates during the visits, so the final discernment can focus on the spiritual call. These matters may include compensation, housing, transition timing, or any unique issues of your church.

4. Stay in touch with your final candidates and consider exploring their feelings about the possible call during these conversations. I have heard several stories of candidates turning down a call at the moment it was offered, but the risk of this disappointment should be minimized if you have followed the general outline of this handbook.

5. When you contact your final candidate, be clear about any contingencies, such as agreeing on a letter of employment and on mutual expectations for the new partnership, as well as any other pending steps, such as completing the background check.

6. Resolve the contingencies.

---

[83] It seems curious that a bishop could need sixty days to judge someone "duly qualified." This is not a holdover from versions of the canons pre-dating the digital age. The 2003 General Convention lengthened the period from thirty to sixty days. In any case, your bishop will not want to delay your transition at this point, and if he or she needs that long to determine that a priest is "duly qualified," you must have a different problem.

7. Ask the vestry to issue the formal call. You will have kept them up-to-date about the search generally and earned their trust in your spiritual discernment. Now you will introduce them to the person God is calling to your church. Prepare meeting handouts or another way to share your excitement. Our committee had updated our vestry monthly about our search process, so at our final meeting with them we used a PowerPoint presentation to remind them of the overall process we had followed and to introduce our new rector. We included his background and pictures of his family and even embedded a few minutes of one of his recent sermons. At the start, the committee was excited and the vestry was curious; by the end of the meeting, the entire room was electrified.

8. Work with your new rector's current bishop to coordinate announcements for the benefit of the church he or she is leaving, since the announcements will start their next rector transition.

Finally, if your new rector is coming from another diocese, he or she must move canonical residency. This involves his or her former diocese providing a Letter Dimissory to your diocese, confirming he or she is a priest in good standing, and your bishop accepting him or her and registering the move with the Secretary of the General Convention of The Episcopal Church. The canons provide ample time for this, and your diocesan transition minister will coordinate it with no work required of you.

The name of your new rector must remain secret until the steps are completed and the rector and his or her current bishop are ready to announce the change to his or her current church. Your search committee and candidates will have avoided leaks throughout the discernment, but your vestry will not be as acculturated to the need for strict confidentiality. Warn them! And move fast through the formal steps.

Discuss Mutual Expectations

The success of the mutual call provides the ideal time for you and your new rector to discuss mutual expectations. You will have touched on most subjects during the discernment, but you should revisit them. The subjects may include worship traditions, how to manage finances, and so forth. **Tool 17** is a list to start your thinking about subjects you want to discuss.

This sort of conversation may be unfamiliar for some clergy, particularly those who began their ministries when leadership was more "top down" and less collaborative than it is becoming in our society. Both the congregation and the new rector have deeply held assumptions about "how we do things." To build a strong partnership, these things should be recognized and discussed.

Agree on Employment Terms

The primary objective of your rector's compensation is to free him or her to focus energy on ministry without the distraction of struggling to meet basic needs. Both the overall compensation package itself and the clarity of agreement about it can limit distractions.

The total compensation includes the salary (or stipend, as The Episcopal Church often calls it), housing or housing assistance, your contributions to the rector's retirement savings, health insurance, other components such as a car or car allowance, and possibly individual considerations, such as tuition assistance for children.

In some cases the rector's spouse works and receives compensation benefits that affect the overall package that you will create for the rector. For example, if the spouse earns excellent family health insurance benefits, it may make sense not to provide health insurance to the rector and to redirect the money to another compensation component.

A caution: I mention income tax matters below only to alert you to them. Base your planning not on this handbook, but on IRS publications and professional tax advisers.[84]

Salary

As with any profession, there are "market rates" of clergy salaries and overall compensation. A market rate considers other Episcopal churches and other Christian churches in your area that have clergy with comparable capabilities and job requirements. Ideally, your vestry, with the aid of your diocese, will have reviewed the compensation package in light of the local market every two or three years. Regardless, this is the moment to ensure that you will pay your new rector equitably.

Paying based on the market is more about equity than about trying to motivate performance. Top professionals in any field do their best mainly for intrinsic rewards, not for compensation, and traditional incentive compensation is increasingly

---

[84] The website of LifeWay Christian Resources has a helpful one-page article by Keith Hamilton that describes key tax issues for clergy.

discredited by behavioral psychologists.[85] Nonetheless, the perceived fairness of compensation plays a big role in the decision to accept a position and to continue in it.

Maybe clergy are less worried about money than the laity, but you want your new rector to feel that your church intends to take good care of him or her and of his or her family. This is not counter to the spirituality of your discernment and call. It is a simple, outward sign of your seriousness.

Retirement Benefits

The Episcopal Church has a defined benefit pension fund for clergy managed by Church Pension Group. Churches are required to contribute to the fund the amount assessed by Church Pension Group under authority in Canon I.8.3. The current pension assessment is 18 percent of clergy salary, other cash compensation, and the value of housing. The pension's assets of $11.5 billion comfortably exceed its actuarially estimated obligations to active and retired priests.[86]

Housing

Housing is quite parish-specific, based on

- the needs of the rector and his or her family;
- your expectations for whether the rector entertains at home;
- your expectations for whether the rector lives near the church, hospitals, other parishioners, and so forth;
- your history and whether you have a rectory; and
- local real estate markets.

If you have a rectory, be sure it is appropriate for a contemporary family and your church's current needs. Review your maintenance plans and any capital project needs. For some churches it may be appropriate to pay all or a portion of certain rectory utility expenses. If this is the case for you, review the utility contracts and recent cost history. Review your property insurance. Some churches with rectories contribute to an equity fund for the rector in order to compensate for the home equity he or she

---

[85] There are many books and studies on the effectiveness of incentive compensation, and *Forbes* magazine's website has a good two-page introduction authored by Donald Delves, "Is Incentive Compensation a True Motivator?"

[86] From footnote 9 to the Financial Statements in the Annual Report of the Church Pension Group, dated March 31, 2018.

might have built by owning a home. Such contributions must be included in the priest's W-2 income as reported to the IRS.

Other churches expect the rector to rent or purchase a home. Renting may make sense if your community has a good selection of rental property. In other communities, home ownership by the rector is the best option. The rector should decide based on the full cost of home ownership, including purchase closing costs, mortgage payments, income that otherwise would be earned on funds used for the down payment, utilities, maintenance, property taxes, homeowners insurance, lawn care time or expense, and the eventual selling expenses, including brokerage commission.

Be aware that income tax considerations of housing are different for clergy. Most rectors qualify to exclude from taxable income the costs of housing, such as mortgage, utilities, and maintenance, as long as the total amount excluded is less than

- the amount of salary designated as "housing allowance" by the vestry in advance of it being paid,
- the rental market value of the housing, and
- the amount of reasonable compensation to the rector.

See Topic 417 at the IRS website for more information on this topic.

The clergy housing exemption began in 1921, soon after the U.S. established an income tax, but it has been attacked in the past twenty years, sometimes by tax reformers who feel it is abused by some "Prosperity Gospel" preachers. Approaches to clergy compensation, including for housing, have evolved in the context of the U.S. Tax Code. We should watch future tax reforms closely to help us determine whether we need to modify further our approaches.

Most clergy, like most Americans, assume home ownership is a good way to build financial equity. Whether they are right depends on

- The full cost of home ownership versus the full cost of rental alternatives and the effects of tax considerations mentioned above.
- At what point in a local residential real estate market cycle the homeowner buys a house, and how long he or she owns it. Housing prices tend to be cyclical based on changes in supply and demand. Smart people can have well informed opinions, but one of the few things economists agree on is that no one can predict future supply and demand, or how to buy at the bottom of a pricing cycle and sell at the

top. A priest buying a home should consider how long he or she expects his or her current employment to last.[87]

- Income tax considerations. Interest on new mortgages currently is tax-deductible for debt up to $750,000, but the income tax analysis is more complicated for clergy, as mentioned above.

As you consider housing for this rector transition, think about both your clergy housing needs twenty years from now and the long-term trends in your local housing market. Rising housing costs in some cities make it increasingly difficult for clergy to afford to buy homes near the church. The problem is acute in places such as New York City and San Francisco, and our vestry has discussed the challenge in Dallas. In addition to residential real estate trends, the details of any future tax reform could have a large bearing on your clergy housing decisions.

Health Insurance

Under the 2009 General Convention Resolution A177, Establishing a Denominational Health Plan, parishes, dioceses, and other Episcopal entities are required to offer health insurance to clergy and lay employees working at least 1,500 hours annually. Church Pension Group offers a variety of medical insurance plans in coordination with leading insurance carriers, and its website has useful resources for parish employees and administrators.

The specific insurance plan(s) your parish and your diocese offer are affected by federal and state laws and state insurance markets. The laws and markets both will keep changing as lawmakers continue to wrestle with the complexities of this huge part of the economy. Church Pension Group monitors this on behalf of The Episcopal Church.

Social Security Tax

In most situations, ministers are considered church employees for federal and state income tax purposes, but for Social Security tax purposes they are treated as self-employed and responsible for their own Social Security Self-Employment taxes (SECA). The SECA tax rate currently is 15.3 percent. For non-clergy employees, churches

---

[87] Nobel Laureate Robert Shiller, one of the world's leading experts on housing economics, proved the common sense idea that the main way to better your odds of a home value increase and lower the odds of a decrease is to own it longer. Marya Alsati-Morad gave a good explanation of this approach on June 24, 2014 in the Indexology Blog.

handle taxes like other employers, withholding half of the tax from employees' gross pay and paying the "employer half," but clergy are responsible for the entire amount themselves.

Some churches reimburse their priests the employer portion of the SECA tax, in which case the reimbursement itself is subject to income taxes and the SECA tax.

Other Benefits

Many churches provide an annual amount for clergy continuing education expenses. Many clergy have strong expectations about this benefit, and it often is documented in their employment agreements.

To help free a rector's energy for ministry, some churches provide financial assistance for childcare or tuition assistance for older children. In the same spirit, a church might assist a rector with matters of care for elderly parents.

Depending on family situation and life stage, many rectors need life insurance and disability insurance, and Church Pension Group offers life and disability insurance options. Your diocese probably has thought through the alternatives.

- If the church pays premiums on group life insurance in excess of the modest amount of $50,000, the excess premiums are treated as additional taxable income of the employee.
- An employer may pay group disability insurance premiums for its employees without including the value in employees' taxable gross income. In this case, any insurance benefits are taxable income when the employee receives them.
- Some employers let employees elect to purchase group disability insurance with after-tax withholding from their gross compensation, in which case any subsequent benefits are not taxable when received.

Like other professionals, most clergy need certain professional advisers, such as an estate planning lawyer and a tax accountant. Depending on your new rector's personal situation, he or she may benefit from other professionals, such as financial planner, psychologist, children's tutors, or healthcare advocate. Probably no one would need every imaginable kind of support, but try to understand the issues that matter to your new rector.

Re-creation and Wellness

A priest in church ministry has enormous potential to serve God and benefit hundreds of parishioners and the tens of thousands whom those parishioners touch. This means it is one of the most physically, mentally, and spiritually demanding roles in our society, and it carries a high risk of burnout. You should plan, budget for, and agree with your rector on the details of

- Time "off-duty" every week.
- Occasional vacations, which include Sundays away from the church.
- A vacation between leaving his or her current congregation and joining you.
- A sabbatical of at least two or three months after five or so years of ministry. Unlike a vacation that is a respite, this period must be long enough for a significant project of personal and vocational renewal.

Some churches provide time and financial support for the rector to go on a brief spiritual retreat every year.

Many successful rectors have spiritual advisers. I have heard of churches covering this expense, while some people hold a philosophical view that any Christian with a spiritual adviser should absorb the related costs personally.

Tool 18 is a worksheet for developing a compensation package and determining the points to cover in a Letter of Agreement on Employment Terms.[88]

Start Your Partnership with the New Rector

Your new rector is joining your lives as well as beginning a ministry partnership with you and diving into an important role in your community.

Announce

The announcement will build excitement among your congregation, church leaders, and community.

Remember, you cannot tell anyone until your new rector tells the congregation he or she is leaving because a leak could make their transition begin with unnecessary

---

[88] See Richard Ullman's "Called to Work Together" for more detailed advice.

disruptions and anxiety. Our vestry and search committee coordinated closely with our new rector. We planned a press release, website changes, and an email to the congregation. We set all the announcement steps in motion one minute after, but not a moment before, the rector told his previous congregation that he had accepted our call.

Tool 19 is a worksheet for planning your announcement.

Welcome

You are welcoming your new rector not only into a job but also into your lives. Make every aspect of the welcome reflect this fact. Realize that the welcome touches the congregation and others as well as the rector and his or her family.

As our vestry and search committee planned to welcome our new rector, we were inspired by the story of Philip and Nathanael being called as disciples. Jesus calls Philip to be a disciple, and Philip tells Nathanael about Jesus. Nathanael asks, "Can anything good come out of Nazareth?" Philip replies simply, "Come and see."[89] Similarly, we felt that the arrival of our new rector was an opportunity to invite friends to church.

You will be excited when the new rector arrives and even those parishioners who are not active in the congregation and other community members will be curious. Use the church's welcome activities to pull them into deeper engagement or re-engagement.

Invite a broad group of lay leaders to coordinate the welcome. The nature of group discernment and the confidentiality concerns of the search will have limited the number of people involved in that work. The welcome provides an opportunity to include more people in key roles and to refresh your lay leadership.

Tool 20 is a worksheet for planning the welcome.

Orient

Helping your rector orient him- or herself is a critical process in building your ministry partnership. The way you have conducted your transition to this point has made a foundation for your ministry together, and the orientation completes the foundation.

Tool 21 is a worksheet for planning the orientation.

---

[89] Excerpted from John 1:43-51.

Build Your Ministry Partnership

In your rector's early months you can be a thoughtful, candid resource as he or she

- becomes a pastor to the congregation;
- understands the church, the strengths you can build on in ministry, and the vulnerabilities;
- works with the congregation for shared understanding of the situation and opportunities,
- identifies goals that might be accomplished early on to build excitement;
- adapts his or her personal style for the greatest effectiveness in your unique church; and
- begins to call on church leaders for support in ministry and to help elevate new leaders.

The vestry should establish a pattern of candid feedback to and from the rector that is regular and comfortable, rather than a special event that causes anxiety because it is rare. Feedback conversations should use mainly descriptive rather than evaluative language. The rector will want to cultivate personal relationships with a few individuals with whom he or she will feel comfortable seeking impressions and insights that help him or her grow in ministry.

You and your rector will find what works for you. The details are specific to your church, and the early months can set the patterns of working together that maximize your potential in ministry together.

Most important, be available. Sometimes search committee and vestry members are tired at this point in the transition, and although they want the church and the rector to flourish, they look forward to a break from their volunteer roles. The future of the church depends on strong follow-through from the members who have led the Ending Stage and the In-between Stage.

Support Others' Transitions

Our committee read many of the available materials and sought advice in conversations with over twenty rectors, bishops, seminary deans, and other church leaders. Much of the most applicable advice we received, however, came from detailed notes made by our church's past search committees, dating back to 1979, and from meeting individually with over twenty members of those committees. Their advice was essential for our recent transition and many of the ideas in this handbook originated with them.

With every step of your path, make good notes for future transitions.

Archive for Your Church

Soon after your new rector arrives, create a digital file with

- Notes from every aspect of your transition. To the extent this handbook's Tools fit your transition, you can include your final draft of each Tool.
- Scanned copies of any paper documents you used if the printed version conveys more than the digital version.
- A memo from each of your committee members, stating what they think worked best in your transition and what advice they would give future transition leaders.

Before saving the documents, expunge everything that would suggest who the candidates or prospective candidates were.

If you used a document sharing system, close the account. Ask the committee members to delete any digital files they have and to give all paper files to one committee member for destruction. Our committee had a Sunday afternoon party where each member placed their files in the committee "Burn Box" for destruction.

I hope your church has good document retention practices so that there will be an obvious place for you to store a flash drive and any paper files. Someone in the church should be designated an appropriate keeper of a digital back-up file.

Share Your Insights

Many of the best innovations of the church originate in parishes, and your transition could serve as an example. Make notes you can share with your diocese and other parishes. Debrief with your bishop and diocesan transition minister, and try to share your experience with the lay leaders of any nearby parishes.

What has helped your congregation become energized and excited about creating your future? What helped your deep mutual discernment discussions with candidates? How did your discernment and other transition work lead toward building a partnership with your new rector?

Consider your experiences in light of the characteristics of your parish and your transition situation. Dioceses may invest a lot of energy in congregations with big, obvious challenges or where the rector-lay partnership has broken down for some reason. Healthy parishes may receive either benign neglect or only as much support as they ask for. Whatever your situation and how your transition has developed, what have you learned that might translate to help others flourish?

Consider how your experience could be relevant to churches with which you share characteristics. If, for example, your church is in an urban downtown, a university town, or a resort area with seasonal population changes, might you have lessons to share that are particular to parishes in similar environments? Lessons from smaller churches would be especially valuable because so many Episcopal churches are small.

There are few shortcuts in a thoughtful transition, yet it is challenging for small congregations to devote the necessary time and financial resources. It would be easy if bishops could simply "give the answers," but that, of course, would be inconsistent with the mutual spiritual discernment that leads to dynamic partnerships between the rector and congregation and would place unrealistic matchmaking expectations on our bishops.

One of the greatest challenges of the clergy deployment system is to achieve the mutual transparency required for deep discernment by both the priests and the parish. This challenge was compounded during our transition due to the breadth of our committee's discernment process with an unusually large number of candidates. I hope you may develop insights that can be useful to other parishes in their discernment dialogues.

Transitions and the Future of The Episcopal Church

I like to think we contemporary Christians have something in common with the early churches at Corinth, Rome and elsewhere. Paul could have given up on them, but he firmly called out their individual behavior and communal divisions and energetically instructed them. Their big potential must have motivated him.

Our potential is enormous. We Episcopalians have weekly worship services reflecting our "three-legged stool" of scripture, reason, and tradition, with lectionary readings that take us through the Bible in a three-year cycle, deeply moving liturgy, sermons that engage our minds and emotions, and especially the Eucharist that mysteriously connects us with God. These gifts of Anglicanism can speak to most contemporary Americans who crave answers to "Why am I here?"

Christianity is challenging to think about, to pray about, and to live. As Ross Douthat explains in a few words in *Bad Religion: How We Became a Nation of Heretics*, "Christianity is a paradoxical religion because the Jew of Nazareth is a paradoxical character. No figure in history or fiction contains as many multitudes as the New

Testament's Jesus."[90] Our three-legged stool has proven to be a powerful framework for trying to know Jesus better.

Anglicanism was born in political controversy over 500 years ago, The Episcopal Church was born in the emotionally charged local divisions between patriots and Tories in the American Revolution, and we have hardly skipped a public controversy all the way through last week. Yet the center has always held through these centuries of wrestling with theological and political disagreements, and our ability to debate and discern in community has enriched our members' spiritual lives and public debates across the world.

Over 20 percent of Episcopal parishes grew by more than 10 percent in the five years to 2014 but based on our strengths, I would expect every parish to be booming.[91] Episcopal membership in 2014 was 1,867,000, or 0.56 percent of Americans, down from its peak of the past century in 1966 of 3,429,000, or 1.7 percent of the population. Pew Research Center surveys in 2015 indicate that more than 3,000,000 Americans identify themselves as Episcopalian or Anglican.[92]

I wish I had the data to test a hypothesis that, over time, declines in parish attendance have occurred predominately during rector transitions. Numerous priests have told me of attendance and programs increasing during their tenure, which makes me suspect that declines happen mainly in the Ending Stage and the In-between Stage of rector transitions and then are recovered under a new rector, but not always to the previous high mark. My anecdotes are not a valid statistical sample, but if this is the case, we have all the more reason to invest effort in achieving excellent transitions.

Regardless of the numbers, my church transition experience and my writing this handbook have led me to an important conclusion. We will be more vibrant overall when we achieve robust clergy-lay partnerships in more churches. We the laity can model the way to those partnerships by how we conduct our rector transitions.

---

[90] Douthat, *Bad Religion, 152. Bad Religion* provides a thought-provoking and readable review of Christianity in America in the past century. It offers deeper understanding for any of us with opinions about why some churches are growing and some have shrunk.

[91] Hadaway, "Episcopal Domestic Facts: 2014."

[92] *Pew Religion & Public Life*, "Religious Landscape Study." I am fascinated that the Pew Research Center has found over a million more Episcopalians than our parishes have enrolled. I hope this means they are at Starbucks on Sunday morning waiting for us to reach out to them. The Pew surveys also report we are America's most highly educated denomination, with the highest incomes. Both characteristics speak to our potential for service.

Project Management for Your Transition

Tool 22 is a worksheet for planning and staying on top of the steps of the transition.

When parishioners say to our search committee members, "You did a great job" it feels good to respond with, "Thank you" although we know the credit is not ours. "The human mind plans the way, but the Lord directs the steps."[93]

I hope this handbook helps you at all times to keep the end in mind, which is to form a productive partnership with your next rector so that your church becomes all it can be. I hope the handbook is adaptable to your unique transition and will help you lead your church with faith and high expectations.

I leave the last word to the writer of Ephesians 3:20-21.

"Now to Him who by the power at work within us is able to accomplish abundantly far more than all we can ask or imagine, to Him be the glory in the church and in Christ Jesus to all generations, forever and ever. Amen."

---

[93] Proverbs 16: 9.

Bibliography

Alban Institute. "Building Blocks: An Anthropological Approach to Congregational Size." *Alban at Duke.* January 16, 2007. https://alban.org/archive/building-blocks-an-anthropological-approach-to-congregational-size/.

Almquist, Curtis, SSJE, interview by author. (April 2015).

Alsati-Morad, Marya. "To Have and to Hold in Residential Real Estate." *www.indexologyblog.com.* June 24, 2014. http://www.indexologyblog.com/2014/06/24/to-have-and-to-hold-in-residential-real-estate/.

American Psychiatric Association Foundation and Faith Community Partnership Steering Committee. "Mental Health: A Guide for Faith Leaders." *Durham Congregations in Action.* 2016. http://www.dcia.org/wp-content/uploads/faith-mentalhealth-guide.pdf.

Antal, James M. *Considering a New Call: Ethical and Spiritual Challenges for Clergy.* Washington, DC: Alban Institute, 2000.

Bass, Diana Butler. *Christianity for the Rest of Us: How the Neighborhood Church Is Transforming the Faith.* New York, New York: HarperCollins, 2006.

Bowen Center for the Study of the Family. 2017. www.thebowencenter.org (accessed July 9, 2018).

Church Pension Group. "2017 Annual Report." *www.cpg.org.* 2017. https://www.cpg.org/linkservid/C522B5B0-A5B1-A2D8-BF37FC195C497AAB/showMeta/0/?label=AboutUs-2017%20Annual%20Report.

—. "DHP Legislation & Plan Model." *www.cpg.org.* https://www.cpg.org/active-lay-employees/insurance/health-and-wellness/denominational-health-plan/resolution-a177/ (accessed January 31, 2017).

—. "Understand Your Assessments." *www.cpg.org.* January 11, 2017. www.cpg.org/active-clergy/retirement/protect-your-benefits/assessments/.

Coffin, William Sloane. *A Passion for the Possible: A Message to U.S. Churches.* Louisville, KY: Westminster/John Knox Press, 1993.

Delves, Donald. "Is Incentive Compensation a True Motivator?" *www.forbes.com.* February 16, 2011. http://www.forbes.com/sites/donalddelves/2011/02/16/is-incentive-compensation-a-true-motivator/#5e9805fb1cac.

Douthat, Ross. *Bad Religion: How We Became a Nation of Heretics.* New York: Free Press, 2010.

Doyle, C. Andrew. *A Generous Community: Being the Church in a New Missionary Age.* New York: Morehouse Publishing, 2015.

Episcopal Church Foundation. *Clergy and Lay Transitions.* August 19, 2016. www.ecfvp.org/vestrypapers (accessed July 12, 2018).

Episcopal News Service. *Jobs & Calls.* August 20, 2016. www.episcopalnewsservice.org/jobs/?type=clergy (accessed July 12, 2018).

Erdy, Susan T., editor. *Episcopal Clerical Directory.* Nashville: Cokesbury, 2017.

Farnham, Suzanne, Joseph P. Gill, R. Taylor McLean, and Susan M. and Ward. *Listening Hearts: Discerning Call in Community.* Harrisburg, PA: Morehouse Publishing, 1991.

Freeman, Lindsay Hardin, editor. *Doing Holy Business: The Best of the Vestry Papers.* New York, New York: Church Publishing, 2006.

Friedman, Edwin H. *Generation to Generation: Family Process in Church and Synagogue.* New York: The Guilford Press, 1985.

Futrell, John Carroll S.J. "Studies in the Spiritualty of Jesuits: Ignatian Discernment (Vol. II no. 2)." *Open Access Journals at Boston College.* April 1970. https://ejournals.bc.edu/ojs/index.php/jesuit/article/viewFile/3560/3153 (accessed July 30, 2018).

Geitz, Elizabeth Rankin. *Calling Clergy: A Spiritual & Practical Guide Through the Search Process.* New York: Church Publishing, Incorporated, 2007.

General Convention of The Episcopal Church. "2009, A177, Amend Canon I.8 [Church Pension Fund] and Establish a Denominational Health Plan." *www.episcopalarchives.org/.* 2009. http://www.episcopalarchives.org/cgi-bin/acts/acts_resolution.pl?resolution=2009-A177.

Green, Thomas H., SJ. *Weeds Among the Wheat: Discernment: Where Prayer and Action Meet.* Notre Dame, Indiana: Ava Maria Press, Inc., 1984.

Griswold, Frank T., interview by author. *Right Reverend and 25th Presiding Bishop of The Episcopal Church* (September 2015).

Gunn, Scott, interview by author. Denver, CO, (February 23, 2016).

Hadaway, C. Kirk. "Age Distribution of Active Priests in Episcopal Congregations in 2015." *www.episcopalchurch.org.* January 11, 2017. www.episcopalchurch.org/library/document/age-distribution-active-priests-episcopal-congregations-2015.

—. "Average Sunday Attendance by Province and Diocese 2005-2015." *The Episcopal Church.* 2016. www.episcopalchurch.org/files/average_sunday_attendance_by_province_and_diocese _2005-2015.pdf.

—. "Episcopal Congregations Overview: 2014." *www.episcopalchurch.org.* January 11, 2017. http://www.episcopalchurch.org/files/episcopal_congregations_overview_2014.pdf.

—. "Episcopal Domestic Fast Facts: 2014." *www.episcopalchurch.org.* http://www.episcopalchurch.org/library/document/domestic-fast-facts-2014 (accessed January 11, 2017).

—. "Episcopal Parish Priests by Diocese, Gender and Position - 2015." *www.episcopalchurch.org.* January 11, 2017. http://www.episcopalchurch.org/library/document/episcopal-parish-priests-diocese-gender-and-position-2015.

—. "New Facts on Episcopal Church Growth and Decline." *The Episcopal Church.* 2015. http://www.episcopalchurch.org/files/new_facts_on_growth_2014_final.pdf.

Hamilton, Keith. "Top six tax mistakes ministers make." *www.lifeway.org.* undated. http://www.lifeway.com/Article/top-six-tax-mistakes-ministers-make (accessed January 31, 2017).

Holbert, John C., and McKenzie, Alyce M. *What Not to Say: Avoiding the Common Mistakes That Can Sink Your Sermon.* Louisville: Westminster John Knox Press, 2011.

Holy Cow Consulting. May 20, 2018. https://holycowconsulting.com/.

Hurst, Anne L., et al. "The State of the Clergy 2012." *www.cpg.org.* 2012. www.cpg.org/linkservid/DC3EE5A8-F95C-2278-107475F87BFDB2AA/showMeta/0/.

Interim Ministries in the Episcopal Church. *IMEC.* August 20, 2016. www.imec-online.org.

—. *IMEC Survey.* August 20, 2016. http://imec-online.org/wordpress/wp-content/uploads/2017/10/TO-Survey-Results.pdf.

Interim Ministry Network. *IMN.* August 20, 2016. http://imnedu.org/.

Internal Revenue Service. "Publication 517 (2015), Social Security and Other Information for Members of the Clergy and Religious Workers." *www.irs.gov.* August 2, 2016. https://www.irs.gov/publications/p517/index.html.

—. "SOI Tax Stats - Individual Income Tax Statistics - 2014 ZIP Code Data." *www.irs.gov.* January 11, 2017. www.irs.gov/uac/soi-tax-stats-individual-income-tax-statistics-2014-zip-code-data-soi.

—. "Topic 417 - Earnings for Clergy." *www.irs.gov.* January 31, 2018. https://www.irs.gov/taxtopics/tc417.

Kahneman, Daniel. *Thinking, Fast and Slow.* New York: Farrar, Straus and Giroux, 2011.

Keirsey, David; Bates, Marilyn. *Please Understand Me: Character & Temperament Types.* Del Mar, CA: Prometheus Nemesis Books, 1978.

Leadership Education at Duke University. *Loren Mead: Still stuck on the importance of the local church.* November 3, 2014. https://livingchurch.org/2014/11/05/mead-conflict-and-creativity/.

Lifeway Research. "Study of Acute Mental Illness and Christian Faith." *www.lifewayresearch.com.* September 2014. http://lifewayresearch.com/wp-content/uploads/2014/09/Acute-Mental-Illness-and-Christian-Faith-Research-Report-1.pdf (accessed July 31, 2018).

Listening Hearts Ministries. *Discernment Listening Guidelines.* http://listeninghearts.org/resources/open-hearts/discernment-listening-guidelines/ (accessed May 26, 2018).

—. *History.* listeninghearts.org/about/history (accessed May 26, 2018).

—. *Signs of the Spirit.* http://listeninghearts.org/resources/open-hearts/spiritual-primer/signs-of-the-spirit/ (accessed May 26, 2018).

Markham, Ian S.; Warder, Oran E. *An Introduction to Ministry: A Primer for Renewed Life and Leadership in Mainline Protestant Congregations.* Chichester, UK: John Wiley & Sons Ltd, 2016.

McCaskill, Robert, interview by author. *Treasurer, Episcopal Diocese of California* (November 2016).

McKenzie, Alyce M., interview by author. *Professor of Preaching and Worship and Director of the Center for Preaching Excellence, Perkins School of Theology, SMU* (November 2015).

McMickle, Marvin A. *Shaping the Claim: Moving from Text to Sermon.* Minneapolis: Fortress Press, 2008.

Mead, Loren B. *A Change of Pastors.* Herndon, Virginia: The Alban Institute, 1986, updated 2005.

—. *The Living Church.* August 20, 2016. www.livingchurch.org/loren-b-mead.

National Council of Churches, 2012 Yearbook of American & Canadian Churches. *Episcopal Church Denominational Profile.* 2012. http://www.thearda.com/Denoms/D_849.asp.

Olsen, Charles M. "Delighted and Disillusioned with Discernment." *Alban at Duke Divinity School.* August 14, 2012. https://alban.org/archive/delighted-and-disillusioned-with-discernment/.

Oswald, Roy M. *New Beginnings: A Pastorate Start Up Workbook.* Washington, DC: The Alban Institute, 1989.

—. *Running Through the Thistles: Terminating a Ministerial Relationship with a Parish.* Lanham, MD: Rowman & Littlefield, 1978.

OTM Board. "An Invitation to the Church." *www.episcopalchurch.org.* December 2016. https://extranet.generalconvention.org/staff/minutes/download?id=1865 (accessed July 12, 2018).

Pew Research Center. "Religious Landscape Study 2014." *Pew Research Center: Religion & Public Life.* May 11, 2015. www.pewforum.org/religious-landscape-study (accessed May 26, 2018).

Phillips, Wm. Bud. *Pastoral Transitions: From Endings to New Beginnings.* Washington, DC: The Alban Institute, 1988.

Price, Matthew, interview by author. *Senior Vice President for Research and Data, Church Pension Group* (October 2015).

Sandel, Dave. "Weeds Among the Wheat: Discernment, Where Prayer and Action Meet, by Thomas H. Green, S.J." *https://davesandel.wordpress.com/.* January 24, 2013. https://davesandel.wordpress.com/2013/01/24/weeds-among-the-wheat-discernment-where-prayer-and-action-meet/ (accessed September 18, 2018).

Schaller, Lyle E. *The Multiple Staff and the Larger Church.* Nashville: Abingdon Press, 1980.

Stannard, Ed. "episopal-life/LHearts." *Episcopal Life Archives.* date unstated. http://arc.episcopalchurch.org/episcopal-life/LHearts.html.

Stevens, R. Paul, and Collins, Phil. *The Equiping Pastor: A Systems Approach to Congregational Leadership.* Lanham, MD: Rowman & Littlefield, 1993.

Sumner, George R., interview by author. *7th Bishop, Episcopal Diocese of Dallas* (July 2015).

SurveyMonkey. www.surveymonkey.com (accessed August 20, 2016).

Sweetser, Thomas P., SJ, and McKinney, Mary Benet, OSB. *Changing Pastors: A Resource for Pastoral Transitions.* Kansas City: Sheed & Ward, 1998.

The Episcopal Church. "2016 Parochial Report." *www.episcopalchurch.org.* http://www.episcopalchurch.org/files/2016_parochial_report_0.pdf (accessed January 31, 2017).

—. *Book of Common Prayer.* 1979.

—. *Cast Wide the Net.* www.episcopalchurch.org/cast-wide-net (accessed July 12, 2018).

—. "Episcopal Church Canons." *The Episcopal Church website.* August 19, 2016. www.episcopalarchives.org/sites/default/files/publications/2015_CandC.pdf.

—. *Sources of Authority.* October 2016. www.episcopalchurch.org/library/glossary/authority-sources-anglicanism.

—. "Studying Your Congregation and Community." *www.episcopalchurch.org.* January 11, 2017. www.episcopalchurch.org/page/studying-your-congregation-and-community.

—. *Transition Ministry.* August 19, 2016. www.episcopalchurch.org/library/office/transition-ministry.

Transition Ministry Conference. January 2017. http://www.transitionministryconference.org/ (accessed July 9, 2018).

Ullman, Richard L. "Called to Work Together." *www.episcopalchurch.org.* 1983, revised 1993. www.episcopalchurch.org/library/document/called-work-together.

Vanderbloemen, William and Bird, Warren. *Next: Pastoral Succession That Works.* Grand Rapids, Michigan: Baker Books, 2014.

Vanderbloemen, William. *Search: The Pastoral Search Committee Handbook.* Nashville, Tennessee: B&H Publishing Group, 2016.

Willimon, William H. *Why leaders are a pain: Truth telling in the parish.* February 8, 2016. https://www.christiancentury.org/article/2016-01/why-leaders-are-pain (accessed May 26, 2018).

Willobee, Sondra B. *The Write Stuff: Crafting Sermons That Capture and Convince.* Louisville: Westminster John Knox Press, 2009.

Wilson, Charles R. *Search: A manual for those called to guide the parish through a process leading to the election of a rector.* Arvada Colorado: Jethro Publications, 1985, updated 1993.

Gratitude

I am grateful for

My parents, Louise and Charles Sheets, whose examples led me into church lay leadership roles.

My remarkable wife, Brenda, and our daughters Blair, Megan, and Anna, who anchor and inspire me daily.

The 2015-16 Rector Search and Transition Committee of Saint Michael and All Angels Episcopal Church – Dallas: Allison Bovard, Joseph Cahoon, Margaret Cervin, Richard D'Antoni, Lee Hobson, Kathy Jenevein, Ben Leal, Christine Paddock, Bob Penn, Jeff Rice, Tricia Stewart, our outstanding senior warden, Matt Waller, and especially my exceptional co-chair, Diana Newton. We all shared a remarkable spiritual journey and became lifelong friends.

Many current and past rectors and associate rectors of Saint Michael and All Angels Church who were invaluable in our transition and influential to this book. In particular, I'd like to thank our new rector, the Rev. Chris Girata; former rectors, the Rev. Bob Dannals and the Rev. Mark Anschutz; recent interim rector, the Very Rev. Doug Travis; former interim rector, the late Rev. Hill Riddle; and associate rectors, the Rev. Tom Blackmon, the Rev. Chip Edens, the Rev. Michael Harmuth, the Rev. Kevin Huddleston, and the Rev. Bill Power.

The insights of numerous leaders of Saint Michael and all Angels Church rector transitions dating back forty years, particularly Tom Luce, Bob Marshall, John McFarland, Sr., Charlie Sartain, Rusty Smith, Nancy Solana, Joan Stansbury, and Stewart Thomas.

Many other leaders who shared their wisdom, particularly the Rt. Rev. Neal Alexander, the Rev. Curtis Almquist, S.S.J.E., Dan Austin, Carolyn Barta, Cynthia Cannon McWhirter, the Very Rev. Kurt Dunkle, Joan Faubion, the Rev. Meghan Froehlich, the Rt. Rev. Frank Griswold, David Konker, the Very Rev. Ian Markham, Bob McCaskill, the Rev. Alyce McKenzie, Barbara Miercort, Bill Novak, the Rt. Rev. Henry Parsley, the Rt. Rev. Claude Payne, the Rev. Ron Pogue, Anne Schmidt, Richard Shaffer, the Very Rev. Rene Somodevilla, the Rt. Rev. George Sumner, Lee Taft, Shelly Vescovo, Kay Whelan, and Ann Woodall.

VTS Press, especially my editor, Dorothy Pearson, and her cheerful adherence to high standards.

The logo on the front cover is owned by Saint Michael and All Angels Church – Dallas and is used with permission.

Finally, I am grateful for the priests who were candidates in our rector search. Each of them is profoundly inspiring. I expect great things from the churches and other institutions they will serve in the coming decades.

Toolbox

Tool 1: Worksheet to Form a Search Committee[1]

Consider prospective search committee members in light of these characteristics or others you develop.

Every member	Some members	Helpful if a member
Devoted to Jesus Christ and has a healthy faith life. Joyful. Discreet. Responsible. Excellent listener. Mature; can discuss hard questions and wait on answers. Projects confidence based on faith. Strongly contributes his or her gifts and resources to the church. Will commit to intensive work through the length of the transition.	In each adult age cohort of the church. Understand each major ministry of the church. In outreach leadership. Understand digital trends. Excellent writer. Consensus developer. Understand the demographic groups where the church would like to grow, for example, adults in their twenties or Spanish language ministries.	Grew up in the congregation. Joined the congregation more recently. Is an adult convert to The Episcopal Church or to Jesus Christ. Has experience working closely with past rectors. Has ties with key local institutions, for example, an Episcopal school.

---

[1] All Tools are also available in digital formats, at www.RectorTransitions.com. You can download and customize them to your church's transition. As with sales of this book, all profits from the sales of the digital Toolkit will be given to Episcopal ministries.

Tool 2: Sample Vestry Charge to a Search Committee

We appoint ___(name all)___ as the members of the ___(name of committee)___. We appoint _____ as ex officio members of the committee.

We charge the Committee to

- Seek the will of God for ___(name)___ Church and this rector transition. Listen to God with an open heart.
- Pray daily for guidance, wisdom, and energy.
- Understand the congregation's dreams, desires, and concerns regarding this transition.
- Work closely with the vestry to lead the parish in imagining what we can become and do during the coming decades.
- Identify candidates to be the next rector of ___(name)___ Church who meet the selection criteria developed together by the vestry and the ___(name of committee)___. Find good candidates wherever they may be.
- Based on deep mutual discernment with the candidates, present to the vestry the person most likely to fit as an exceptional rector and partner in ministry for the next stage in our history.
- Plan your work carefully and conduct it prayerfully, thoroughly, and with alacrity.
- Work closely with the vestry, provide regular updates of your progress, and work within timelines and budgets as agreed upon with the vestry.
- Support the vestry in its work through the transition, including any interim period between the present rector's last day with the parish and such time as the next rector arrives and is integrated into the parish.
- Seek the counsel and support of the Bishop of ___(name)___ through the search, discernment, and call process.
- Maintain strict confidentiality regarding candidates and discernment discussions.
- Comply with
  - the Constitution and Canons of The Episcopal Church,
  - the Constitution and Canons of the Diocese of ___(name)___, and
  - The Articles of Incorporation, By-laws, Policies and procedures of __(name)__ Church.

Tool 3: Frequently Asked Questions (FAQs) Worksheet

You must be vague about some matters to maintain confidentiality, but being specific where possible will help earn the congregation's trust in the process and your leadership.

Use judgment regarding your church's situation. In an effort to engage the congregation, you might proactively answer some questions before they are asked. On the other hand, some questions reflect anxiety, and you may decide to answer only the people who ask them rather than address those answers to the whole congregation.

Likely parishioner questions early in the transition	Thoughts on responses
Why is the outgoing rector leaving?	Many parishioners who have this question may not voice it. Conspiracy theories can arise in even the most normal situations, so it is good to refer to the previous rector's call to another ministry or to be brief but clear and honest if the reason is less comfortable, assuming there are not legal reasons for silence. The emotional connection with a rector usually is intense, so it would be naïve to think you can gloss over the previous rector's departure. The congregation will need to process the news.
How long will the transition take?	Early in the transition parishioners may be anxious about the church losing momentum and want assurances that the transition will be brief. You probably are not in a position to guarantee speed, so you should explain how key responsibilities are in good hands during the interim period. Explain why it takes time to conduct a thorough search. Tell them what you assume about the timeline, but take care not to over-promise. You don't want to cause anxiety if delays occur that are beyond your control. If the church is healthy in terms of relationships, the state of ministries, and finances, and is free of conflicts, you should be able to do each step of the transition as fast as you can do it well.

Likely parishioner questions early in the transition	Thoughts on responses
What are the steps in the search for a new rector?	Some parishioners may be familiar with recruiting in business and other secular arenas, so you may need to convey that a rector search involves some of the same administrative tasks, but the candidates and the search committee will be in mutual discernment to understand God's call, which is not the typical secular process.
	Describe the planning and steps the committee is taking to prepare for discernment.
	Describe listening sessions, the parish survey and anything else you plan to engage everyone's thoughts on the transition. Announcing dates for listening sessions is a good example of specificity that builds trust.
	Explain how the committee will describe your church to prospective candidates through various means as discussed below.
	Mention that the committee will get to know candidates in stages, from their written OTM Clergy Profile, other written exchanges, phone or videoconference interviews, and intensive personal meetings.
Why is the search confidential?	Explain that the committee is never allowed to discuss whether any priest will be, is, or was a candidate or talk about any aspect of the discernment discussions with any candidate. It would be devastating to a candidate's relationship with his or her present church if it were known that he or she entertained leaving them.
Who is leading the search?	Share short biographies of the search committee members. Explain how the committee and the vestry are coordinated and that, ultimately, the elected vestry will call the new rector.

Likely parishioner questions early in the transition	Thoughts on responses
How do we find candidates?	Tell them that the best way to identify candidates is for parishioners to recommend priests who have impressed them. Assure them that the committee is seeking referrals from leaders in the diocese and beyond.
How can parishioners identify possible candidates, make other suggestions, or ask questions and make comments?	Create an email in-box and a physical in-box at the church. If some committee members prefer not to publish personal phone numbers and email addresses online, you need to set church email addresses that are confidential or a committee email address, for example, rector.transition@(TheChurch.org). Our committee advertised that email and snail mail would be forwarded automatically to the committee co-chairs and shared with the full committee but with no one else.
Will we have an interim rector?	*The answer depends on your church's plans.*
What will happen to the staff? *You do not have to answer this question unless it is asked, but don't be surprised by it.*	It is typical for a new rector to assess all clergy and lay staff after becoming integrated into the church, and sometimes this assessment leads to changes. If it is true, you can add that, based on what you know today, you do not anticipate changes.
What is the role of the bishop and diocese?	Episcopal canons (church laws) require the bishop's approval for a church to call a candidate to be its rector. Add that your bishop and diocesan transition minister have been helpful and are being updated throughout the search process.
What are we looking for in a rector?	First, answer this by announcing listening sessions. Later, you might post a summary of the committee's specifications for the position.

Likely parishioner questions early in the transition	Thoughts on responses
Is _____ eligible to be our rector?	All ordained Episcopal or Anglican priests in good standing and under the age of seventy-two are eligible, regardless of background or where they work now. Whether particular priests are interested depends on how they discern God's call for the next years in their vocation and how they come to understand us through the parish profile we develop. The search committee will be inclusive in identifying candidates and will follow the Holy Spirit's guidance as to who could be the best fit for the next stage of the church's future.
Additional FAQs, later in the transition	
What is the transition status now?	*The answer depends on when you update your FAQs.*
How many candidates do we have?	This calls for polite deflection, as in "We can't say how many, but one of the most gratifying aspects of the search is to see firsthand how many excellent priests the church has, and to know that some of them are interested in us."
When will we call the new rector?	*The answer depends on what you feel is appropriate to say, if anything.*
	Remind parishioners that the essence of the search is for the committee and the candidates to listen to the Holy Spirit. Invite parishioners to join you in praying for the parish, the process, and your future rector. Refer to the parish prayer that you developed for the transition.

Tool 4: Questions to Start a Forward-Looking Assessment

Assess your ministries. What is working well or badly? Why do you judge it this way?	• Is your worship meaningful to all members? Does it attract visitors to become engaged members? What is wonderful about it? • Which small groups are essential to fellowship and friendships among parishioners? • What does your church offer your community? • Assess your Christian formation for children and for adults. • How do you share Jesus Christ and invite people to join your church? • What are your important outreach efforts? Whom do you serve and how do they benefit? Who among your congregation is engaged in outreach? • What are the roles of music and other arts in the life of the church? • Which of your traditions animate the congregation? Which are habits that may no longer fit?
Understand your community and how it may have changed since your church's last transition.	• What opportunities does your community offer your church? • Is your community multicultural and multilingual? • What are the population and income levels, and are they growing or shrinking? • Consider other local churches and what is going well or badly with them.
What are your church's key relationships in the community?	• What is your engagement in your diocese? • What is important about relationships with other institutions? schools? other churches? nonprofit agencies? local government? your neighborhood? seminaries? Episcopal and Anglican organizations?

Understand your clergy and lay staffing.	• Which church needs are met very well and which are not fully met by your current staffing? • What strengths can the new rector build on, and where are staffing or performance gaps that hold the church back? This is complex to understand and the perspective of lay leaders is only one slice of a 360-degree view.
What is the state of your finances and facilities?	• Most churches' annual giving reflects a variation of the 80/20 Rule, with some minority of the congregation representing a majority of annual giving. What does this equation look like for your parish? • What are your debt and cash reserve situations? • What have the roles of lay leaders and clergy been in raising annual revenue? • What are the ongoing and one-time maintenance needs of your facilities? • How would you assess your last capital campaign?
How are you living into the digital age? The Rev. Scott Gunn, Executive Director of Forward Movement, has observed, *"If you do not have a strong digital presence, or if it is not geared to mobile devices, for people under thirty-five your church does not exist."*	• Do you use social media and an engaging website to serve your congregation and others and to evangelize? • In church programming and event planning, do you take into account how the web is influencing how we learn and connect with each other? • Do you curate Christian formation materials for your congregation from the many resources available on the web? • How is your church alive digitally? Digital natives (generally, people under thirty-five) live out their relationships on the web as well as in the physical world. The web is not just another place to communicate things historically communicated in print but also a place where people interact.

What sort of rector-church partnership are you completing with your outgoing rector?	• Whether he or she has had a long energetic tenure or is the third rector in six years, why? If the relationship has been marked by divisions or by consensus, why? • How has your outgoing rector changed, and how has the partnership changed in the past few years? • If your outgoing rector were to remain, in what ways would he or she fit and/or not fit your needs in the next few years?
How do you measure your church's results? We cannot track individuals' spiritual health on spreadsheets, but there are ways to measure church vibrancy.	Sample measurable goals include • new members attracted, • adult confirmations, • mission program events, • involvement in small groups, • worship attendance, • hits on particular pages of the church website, year over year, • traffic on church social media sites, • visitors on Sundays and holidays and at church events, • engagement in each church ministry, and • annual giving per household compared to Internal Revenue Service data on average household income in the zip codes where parishioners live.[2]

---

[2] The IRS shows data on adjusted gross income averages by zip code, in downloadable spreadsheets at https://www.irs.gov/uac/soi-tax-stats-individual-income-tax-statistics-2014-zip-code-data-soi.

Tool 5: Worksheet to Prompt Parish Survey Questions

Categories of questions	Sample questions[3]
Respondent demographics	<ul><li>Age</li><li>Gender</li><li>Marital status</li><li>Number of children at home</li><li>Years as a member of the church</li><li>Baptized?</li><li>Confirmed?</li><li>Cradle Episcopalian?</li><li>Zip code</li><li>Travel time from home to church</li><li>Military veteran?</li><li>Education level</li></ul>
Involvement	<ul><li>Why are you a member of our church?</li><li>Which church ministries are you involved in?</li><li>How frequently do you attend our worship services?</li><li>In which of the following ways do you support the church financially?</li><li>In the past _____ years, has your involvement increased, decreased, or stayed the same?</li><li>What is the main reason for your change in involvement?</li><li>In the next _____ years, would you like your involvement to increase, decrease, or stay the same?</li></ul>

---

[3] Offer multiple choices. Use a range if necessary, for example, for age or years as a parishioner.

Categories of questions	Sample questions[3]
Worship	• Ask respondents to rate the importance of worship service components such as music, liturgy, ritual, and preaching. • Ask them to rate the quality of the various aspects of worship.
Church ministries such as worship, outreach, and Christian formation. *Subjects you raised in **Tool 4** may belong in the survey.*	• Rate the following ministries as Very Effective, Effective, Somewhat Effective, or Ineffective. • Rate the following ministries as Needs More Emphasis, Generally Satisfied, Very Satisfied, or Receives Too Much Emphasis. • Which of the following new ministries do you think we Definitely Should Start, Should Consider Starting, Should Not Start?
Views on significant issues the congregation faces	These questions likely are highly specific to your church. They may involve particular opportunities or threats, surprising new developments, and so forth. If you need to explore a subject, it must be obvious.
Qualities of the next rector *By asking about more qualities than most parishioners may have considered, these questions can help respondents to think broadly about the rector's role.*	Rank the following qualities our next rector might have as Very Important, Important, Somewhat Important, or Unimportant. *The Handbook section, "Understand the Role of a Rector" and Tool 9 both provide sample qualities to list.*

Categories of questions	Sample questions[3]
Feelings and ideas	These examples seek comments rather than data: • One thing I hope will never change about our church is… • A change that would be good for our church is… • I am proud of our church because… • What worries me most about our church is… • My greatest dream for our church is…

Tool 6: Transition Budget Worksheet

	Amount
Revenue *(The dollar amounts are merely examples.)*	
Funds from parish budget, savings, or endowment	$30,000
Parishioner donations to the transition effort (*Funds raised without cannibalizing annual giving.*)	20,000
Total revenue	**$50,000**
Expenses	
Celebrating the era that is ending *(Activities include parties, a gift for the outgoing rector, etc.)*	$2,000
Transition administrative expenses *(This may include a document management system subscription, parish survey expenses, printing of communications materials, website support, expenses of corresponding with candidates, etc.)*	2,000
Search consulting	2,000
Marketing materials for search *(This could include an individualized parish profile and informational packages for candidates.)*	2,000
Candidate visits to us *(Examples include travel expenses of candidates and spouses, plus local meals for them and committee members.)*	8,000
Visits to candidates *(Costs incurred include airfare, hotel, and meals for a team from the committee to visit each candidate.)*	15,000
New rector moving expenses	10,000
New rector housing set-up *(These costs could include mortgage down payment assistance, brokerage fees, and other costs, depending on the compensation agreement.)*	5,000

New rector welcome events *(Sample events include parties and a formal service, i.e., The Institution of a New Rector, from page 559 of the Book of Common Prayer.)*	2,000
New rector orientation activities *(Plan and budget for the new rector to meet the congregation personally and to be oriented to the community expeditiously.)*	2,000
Total expenses	**$50,000**
The downloadable version of this Tool provides more detail to help you to plan the timing of revenue and expenses.	

Tool 7: Practical Advice on Confidentiality

Specific concern	Prepare to protect confidentiality
Parishioners ask a committee member the status of priests they know. Dozens of our large church's former associate rectors could have been considered rector candidates, so we heard this question often.	Practice responses such as, "I can't confirm or deny whether any individual priest is or has been in discussions with us." Early in the search you might respond, "It would be inappropriate for me to answer, but do you think (name) could be a good candidate for us?" Perhaps the most gracious non-answer is, "One of the most gratifying aspects of the search is to see how many wonderful clergy the church has."
A question comes from a friend in a setting that catches us off guard.	Some search committee members prepare for this risk by deliberately talking about the search with a close friend in order to become comfortable drawing the line between sharing appropriate search process information and not sharing any information.
A parishioner asks a committee member's spouse about the search.	Do not discuss candidate names or details of the search with spouses so they can honestly say they don't know.
Keeping the many sensitive files related to a search confidential but accessible to committee members.	Some committees restrict file copies to a locked "reading room" at the church. Our committee wanted the convenience of online files, so we subscribed to Dropbox for Business (currently $12.50 per user per month for a one-year subscription). One member served as system administrator, and the account logins were set for two-step verification. At the end of the search, the software wiped the files from all the personal devices we used to access them. Both Apple and Google offer alternatives for secure file sharing.

Specific concern	Prepare to protect confidentiality
A committee member loses a laptop or smartphone with committee files on it.	Password protect your devices. Never send candidate names or information by email, which could be read on a lost device. If you use a secure online file system, the administrator can lock out a lost device so it can no longer access files on the system.
A committee member's spouse or executive assistant has access to his or her emails about the search.	Every committee member must set up a secure private email box so that all emails related to the transition are confidential.
Someone might overhear a search committee meeting.	Establish meeting locations where no one can hear you or see any flipcharts or other visual materials you use.
Someone overhears committee members talking outside a meeting.	Many committees create code names to avoid using candidates' names.
A parishioner hears about a committee member's travel and guesses who may be a candidate. This risk is greater when you visit a small town with one Episcopal priest than if you visit a large city.	Don't discuss your travel during the search. Seemingly harmless anecdotes can start damaging rumors.
A priest who is extremely close to a search committee member asks or speculates about candidates.	Don't discuss candidates with a priest who is not on your committee or serving as a candidate's reference. I've heard numerous anecdotes about leaks in a number of churches' searches, and have been surprised that in the majority of these, a priest had shared information that a search committee member had told him or her.

Specific concern	Prepare to protect confidentiality
A candidate leaks that he or she is a candidate. Our committee was surprised when more than one priest's candidacy was leaked when candidates shared with clergy friends and with lay friends in our church.	When queried in such a situation, say, "Others may share secrets they are privy to or speculate about who may be a candidate, but it is not appropriate for me to confirm or deny." Obviously this cannot reverse a leak, but it can politely stop the conversation without the risk that you may divulge more than the candidate did.
You contact a reference identified by a candidate, and the reference knows one of your other candidates.	Do not mention the candidate who did not provide this reference, unless the reference is the two candidates' current bishop with whom both would be having candid conversations regarding this discernment.
After the new rector has arrived, someone asks a search committee member about his or her discussions with a candidate.	A search committee member cannot explain the complex discernment process to someone who was not present, even after the process has concluded. Never breach the confidentiality.
Ten years after the search someone asks about a candidate who was not called.	Search members must never discuss a candidate and risk affecting his or her relationships with current or past parishioners.

Tool 8: Sermon Listening Sheet

Questions	Write your reactions to the sermon
What was the claim of the sermon (the "what")? How would you summarize the thesis in a sentence?	
How did the sermon's claim grow out of the biblical text?	
How did the sermon engage you (the "so what")?	
How did the preacher use emotion? How did he or she use stories, humor, and rhetorical tools such as conflict and imagery?	
What response did the sermon ask of you (the "now what")?	
Form: Did the opening pull you in and introduce the theme? Did the sermon unfold clearly so you could follow the thread? How did the preacher "stick the landing?"	
Describe the sermon with a few adjectives, such as teaching, inspiring, thought provoking, or pastoral.	
What, if anything, did you learn about the preacher?	
How did the sermon fit this congregation?	

Tool 9: Rector Qualities Worksheet

Qualities *You may have other categories.*	*Describe the qualities you seek. The following are examples.*
Pastor	Distinguish personal pastoral gifts from the candidate's approach to managing pastoral care of a congregation. Approachable pastoral demeanor and communication. Motivated to serve others for reasons other than a personal need for validation.
Leader	Builds trust. Thinks strategically about church direction and initiatives. Visionary and builds support for the vision. Organizes execution and follows through. Works well as a member and a leader of teams. Various leadership styles can be effective. Would a particular one work best for our church?
Preacher	Touches parishioners' hearts from the pulpit, and touches their minds with content and delivery that fits us. Consistent from week to week. Makes visitors want to come back for more.
Character	Behaves with integrity. Respectful. Inclusive. Has a sense of his or her strengths and weaknesses. Confident yet humble.
Spiritual guide	Has an active prayer life. Can give spiritual guidance. Maintains life balance.
Intellect	Smart, curious, well educated, and creative.
Communicator	Listens well. Communicates in small and large groups. Understands the audience. States thoughts clearly.
Personality	Enjoys and uses humor. Emotionally grounded. Warm. Has gravitas but does not take him- or herself too seriously. Energetic. Has diverse and meaningful personal interests.
Personal chemistry	Seems likely to fit with us and our community.
Potential to grow with us	Lifelong learner, open to advice. Has a foundation of experience in life and as a priest that will enable him or her to be a strong partner.

Qualities *You may have other categories.*	*Describe the qualities you seek. The following are examples.*
Specific experience or knowledge we need	*Depends on unique characteristics of the church.*
Spouse, if applicable	Can relate well with a wide range of parishioners. Personally mature and grounded. Would fit in our parish comfortably. Discreet. Seems to have a mutually supportive marriage.

Tool 10a: Parish Profile Worksheet

This list is designed to help you collect background information before you write anything. The material itself will suggest how you organize the presentation to tell your story. Include photos! Include numbers. Be precise. Rather than saying, "We have weekly Bible studies," say, "Four Bible study groups meet weekly and draw over 30 participants in aggregate every week." The downloadable version incorporates Tool 10b in case you want to work on a profile and your Ministry Portfolio in tandem.

Profile information	Thoughts on content and presentation
Use photographs throughout the profile	Ask parishioners for pictures of parish people and events that can convey a sense of your parish.
Summary statements about "who we are"	If your parish has a written Vision, Mission, Statement of Values, or other statements of who you are, start your Profile with them. If you want to develop such statements but haven't yet, you probably should wait to do it in partnership with your new rector.
Introduction	This should be easy to write after the other sections are completed.
History	The intent here is not to dwell in the past but to use history to help parishioners and candidates alike understand how key experiences and people have shaped the congregation's present DNA.
Worship	How would you describe your regular worship experience every week and during holidays? What are the roles of the priest and lay volunteers such as ushers, acolytes, and lectors? Describe the music and other arts. How are visitors identified and welcomed?
Christian formation	How do you educate children and encourage the spiritual journey of adults? Include your classes, small Bible study groups, programs you curate from others' online content, and so forth. What are the objectives of each of the programs? How do you measure their success?

Profile information	Thoughts on content and presentation
Pastoral care	How does the parish meet the special needs of individuals and families? What are the roles of clergy and of lay volunteers? What special programs, such as addiction recovery, family counseling, and Eucharistic visits, do you have? What is the role of prayer ministries?
Outreach	What are your initiatives to serve beyond your walls? Whom do you serve? Who participates? How does outreach shape your congregation?
Fellowship	What groups and activities encourage Christian fellowship? What are your regular small groups?
Staff	List the staff and their responsibilities. Describe the routine processes that get everything done.
Leadership	What portion of the congregation is active in leading the parish's ministries and in what ways? Where does the vestry focus its energy? What committees and regular meetings does the parish depend on? Discuss how ministry initiatives typically have developed in terms of a partnership between the rector and the congregation.
Facilities	Describe your buildings and campus and how you optimize their use.
Finances	Summarize your annual revenue and expenses. What are the trends in number of households pledging each year and the average amount? Do you have an endowment or other key financial assets?
Diocese	Talk about your bishop and diocesan staff members who are involved with your parish. How does your parish participate in the diocese?
City and region	Describe the area in terms of people, geography, important institutions, the economy, and social trends. You may get ideas from other sources, such as a Chamber of Commerce, but remember to adapt the information to your audience. Describe how your parish fits among local churches.

Profile information	Thoughts on content and presentation
Survey results	If you have done a parish survey for your transition, highlights those data and comments, as applicable, in the sections of your profile.
Dreams for the future	Don't stop at describing who you are now. Share your emerging consensus about what the congregation aspires to become.
Special challenges the parish faces	Focus on any challenges that are particular to your church rather than those shared by most churches.
What are you looking for in your next rector?	Summarize desired rector qualities. (See **Tool 9**.)
How can prospective candidates and others contact the search committee?	What materials does the committee require for a priest to become a candidate? List the members, and provide email contact information for the committee.

Tool 10b: OTM Ministry Portfolio Worksheet

Data field[4]	Thoughts on presentation[5]
Parish and Address	
Position	Rector.
Receiving Names Until	You need a deadline to manage your discernment process, but may change it if necessary after your initial posting or even decide to extend the deadline for individual candidates. For example, our committee granted an extension for a priest who was delayed by a family emergency.
Contact	List an email address for the committee or member(s) designated as the first contact.
Weekly Average Sunday Attendance (ASA)	The ASA data reported in your past ten annual parochial reports are also visible to candidates at The Episcopal Church's website.[6]
Number of Weekend Worship Services	
Number of Weekday Worship Services	
Number of Other per Month Worship Services	
Current Annual Compensation	Some may consider this field confidential or not relevant to candidates whose experience and qualifications may be different from their outgoing rector.

---

[4] As used by the OTM in January 2016.

[5] Your diocesan transition minster can authorize one committee member to log in to the OTM system to cut and paste the language you develop here. You may need or choose to leave some fields blank.

[6] "Studying Your Congregation and Community."

Data field[4]	Thoughts on presentation[5]
Cash Stipend	Secular organizations call this the salary. I strongly believe we should pay clergy well, but I question whether your initial salary estimate should be one of the first filters through which a prospective candidate views your position. I also worry that emphasis on the salary at the outset of the search could focus a committee on limits instead of on God's abundance and the healthy parish finances that can result from a great fit between rector and congregation. You could say "Stipend commensurate with qualifications in the context of overall compensation." If you state a range, expect candidates to remember the top of the range more than the bottom. Since the OTM's Ministry Portfolio focuses heavily on compensation components, our committee stressed that we intended to pay well and looked forward to developing a comprehensive compensation program that fit the rector we would call, but we did not provide specific numbers.
Housing/Rectory Detail	Describe the housing support you provide, for example, a rectory, a housing fund, or mortgage support. Some parishes state an amount here.
Utilities	This could apply if you have a rectory.
SECA Reimbursement	This field refers to Social Security Self Employment Tax. For purposes of Social Security (versus other tax and legal purposes), clergy are not treated as employees whose Social Security tax is withheld. Instead, clergy must pay the IRS 15.3 percent of their salary plus housing support (or in the case of a rectory, the rental value). Episcopal parishes typically reimburse the rector either one half of the tax (which amounts to 7.65 percent of applicable compensation) or a set amount.
Compensation Available for New Position	This question apparently applies to newly created positions.

Data field[4]	Thoughts on presentation[5]
Housing Available for	This field describes the size of family that the rectory can accommodate.
Pension Plan	Confirm your compliance with Church Pension Fund requirements. Mention if you provide other retirement savings benefits.
Healthcare Options	Summarize the healthcare insurance coverage you offer in compliance with Resolution A177 of the 76th General Convention in 2009.
Dental	Does the health insurance cover dental?
Housing Equity Allowance in Budget	Yes or no.
Annual Equity Amount	
Vacation Weeks	
Vacation Weeks Details	Some parishes specify how many Sundays are included in vacation weeks.
Continuing Education Weeks	
Continuing Education Weeks Details	
Continued Education Funding in Budget	
Sabbatical Provision	
Travel/Auto Account	Many parishes reimburse the rector for the travel expenses of pastoral duties and travel to diocesan meetings and the like.
Other Professional Account	Many parishes have a Rector's Discretionary Fund for confidential pastoral purposes with a written policy for how it is governed. Some have entertainment accounts.
Additional Compensation Note *(The form does not ask for this but allows space to include a note.)*	We wrote that our parish was "flexible to shape a comprehensive compensation package, including the components addressed by the OTM, and possibly others that may be desired, for example, children's tuition assistance, elderly parent care, and so forth."
Long form questions	*You likely can excerpt from your individualized parish profile to answer all of these questions.*

Data field[4]	Thoughts on presentation[5]
Describe a moment in your worshiping community's recent ministry, which you recognize as one of success and fulfillment.	
How are you preparing yourself for the church of the future?	
Please provide words describing the gifts and skills essential to the future leaders of your worshiping community.	
Describe your liturgical style and practice for all types of worship services provided by your community.	
How do you practice incorporating others in ministry?	
As a worshiping community, how do you care for your spiritual, emotional, and physical well-being?	
How do you engage in pastoral care for those beyond your worshiping community?	
Describe your worshiping community's involvement in either the wider Church or geographical region.	
Tell about a ministry that your worshiping community has initiated in the past five years. Who can be contacted about this?	
What is your practice of stewardship, and how does that shape the life of your worshiping community?	
What is your worshiping community's experience of conflict? And how have you addressed it?	
What is your experience leading/addressing change in the church? When has it gone well? When has it gone poorly? And what did you learn?	
Prior Incumbents *(Spaces asking the names, titles, start dates and end dates of the last three senior ministers.)*	
Church School	If you have a school, insert highlights from how you described it in your individualized parish profile.
Number of Teachers/Leaders for Church School	
Number of Students for Children School	Number and age range.

Data field[4]	Thoughts on presentation[5]
Number of Teachers/Leaders for Teen/Young Adults School	
Number of Students for Teen/Young Adults School	Number and age range.
Number of Teachers/Leaders for Adults School	
Number of Students for Adults School	Number and age range.
Day School	
Number of Students for Day School	Number and age range.
Number of Teachers for Day School	
Number of Total Staff for Day School	
Worshiping Community Website	
Media Links	List any related websites, social media pages, and handles, such as Facebook, Twitter, Instagram and Pinterest; video and audio channels such as YouTube, Vimeo and Livestream; event scheduling sites such as Eventbrite or Picatic; any online publication platforms such as Issuu; and publications with their own sites.
Online References	
Languages Significantly Represented	
Provide Worship or Classes in Which Languages	
Bishop	Include email address and phone for contacts.
Diocesan Transition Minister	
Current Warden/Board Chair	

Data field[4]	Thoughts on presentation[5]
Previous Warden/Board Chair	
Search Chair	
Parish/Institution	
Local Community Leader	I recommend not answering this due to confidentiality concerns. You can introduce your final candidates to a community leader later if it seems advisable.

Tool 10c: Open Positions Form, Transition Ministry Conference[7]

Parish and Position	
Date Posted	
Diocese	
Location	
Position Type	Full-time, part-time, or other.
Position Details	
Setting	City, town, rural, etc.
Compensation	Some show a dollar amount, or write "competitive."
Health Benefits	Respond in a few words, for example, "full family."
Housing	Typically either the housing allowance or what size family the rectory can accommodate.
Equity Allowance	Yes or no. Some parishes pay into a savings fund for a rector to buy a house when he or she retires.
Parish Profile	
Communicants in Good Standing	Number.
Average Sunday Attendance	Number.
Child Population in Church School	Number.

[7] Applies to parishes whose dioceses are in the Transition Ministry Conference. You can view others' listings at jobs.transitionministryconference.org/.

Adult Population in Church School	Number.
Budget	Dollar amount.
Worship Style (presented in a list of statements for a Yes or No response)[8]	
Strengths	Respond in one paragraph and refer to your parish website and parish profile.
Challenges	Respond in one paragraph.
Comments	Respond in one paragraph or offer a few bullet points about characteristics of the person you seek.
Contact Information	Provide a name with email and possibly phone contact information, and state what materials are required to formally enter discernment with you.

---

[8] The choices include: Anglo-Catholic, Broad Church, Charismatic, Contemporary, Emergent, Morning Prayer, Non-traditional, Prayer Book, Renewal, Rite I, Rite II.

Tool 11: Sample Prospect Summary

Information	Example
Name	The Rev. Jane Jones Smith.
Current Position and Dates	Associate Rector, St. Thomas – Lexington, AK, 2011-present.
Contact	Cell phone or private email address, if known. It may be difficult to contact him or her confidentially at church.
Ministry/Work History	Seminarian at Trinity – Davis, 2010-11. High school Spanish teacher 14 years before seminary.
Spouse or Partner, Profession	John Smith, CPA and sculptor.
Children and Dates of Birth	John, Jr., (date of birth); Susan, (date of birth).
Education	M.Div., CDSP; B.A. in Spanish, UC-Davis.
Community and Diocesan Roles	Hosts weekly 30-minute local radio program. Diocese of Alaska mission committee.
Sermons	www.saintthomasalaska.org/sermons
Publications	Gran Libro de la Poesía Española (editor, Spanish poetry book) Blog on evangelism: http://motherjaneofthenorth.blogspot.com
Info on Current Position	ASA 130 in 2015, steady increase from 85 in 2009-10. Budget $550k (pledge and plate $500k + endowment income.) Led $800k capital campaign to build new parish hall.
Other	Prospect's date of birth.

Tool 12: Worksheet to Track Candidates

The downloadable version allows you to track all prospects and candidates clearly on one page using landscape orientation. The format cannot fit on a handbook page, so this version merely shows what could be included.

List **Prospects and Candidates**, and the following information in five columns, with a row for each priest.	List **Status in the Process**, and the following information in eight columns to the right of the five columns described on the left.
Name	**Have we written a Prospect Summary?** Yes or no.
Current position, for example, Associate Rector.	**Has this priest been invited into mutual discernment?** If yes, include the date and whether by letter, email, or phone.
Current church and description, including parish name and location. You may want to note descriptors such as its ASA and annual budget.	**How has the priest responded?** Yes, no, or "praying about it."
Personal description, noting characteristics you consider essential or desirable. For example, you might note, "Can conduct worship in French."	**Assigned Shepherd** Name of committee member, if any, who is assigned as the lead contact with the priest.
Suggested by – Record who suggested this priest so you can thank them or contact if you have a question for them.	**Summary of Follow-up Contacts** Enter a few words about each interaction. Who had it? Date?
	Is the formal file complete? Yes or no, and what is missing.
	Notes on Discernment Discussion Administrative notes only e.g. about schedules and files, not notes on the substance of discussions.
	Notes for Follow-up The next steps in discernment or contact with the priest.

Tool 13a: Sample Invitation into Mutual Discernment

Dear Rev. _____ :

We are in a search for the ___20th (or insert your number)___ Rector of _____
Episcopal Church in __(city)___ , ___(state)___ , and you have been recommended to us as
a potential candidate. We encourage you to read our parish profile at ___(website
address)___ , review our posting with the Office for Transition Ministry, and prayerfully
consider entering into discernment with us.
(Insert a brief paragraph describing unique aspects of the parish.)
(Insert a brief paragraph describing the parish's dreams for the future.)
(Insert a brief paragraph describing the rector you are seeking and praying for.)
(Insert a brief paragraph on what is required to become a candidate. For example, our
committee wrote:

> We encourage you to pray about whether you may be the right person
> to lead us as we fulfill our potential, and we may be the parish where
> you can be your best for God. If you feel called to mutual discernment,
> we invite you to join this holy process with us by providing your
> resume, a cover letter discussing your potential fit as our next Rector,
> and your complete OTM Clergy Portfolio.)

Alternatively, if you know someone whom you believe might be a good fit, please share
this in hopes that he or she will consider entering into discernment with us.
We look forward to hearing from you. We are praying for you!

With blessings,
[Signed by the committee chair(s)]

Tool 13b: Sample Email Welcoming into Mutual Discernment

Dear Rev. _____,

We are grateful that you are entering discernment with us and look forward to getting to know each other well.

We have received everything we need from you at this point. We expect to receive applications through _(date)_ and will begin our internal discussions then.

Our next step will be to ask some candidates for _(more information, phone conversations, video interviews, something else?)_.

We expect to be back in touch with you by _(approximate date)_. If you have questions for us at any time please contact us by _(email address and/or phone number)_.

In the meantime we are praying for your ministry in _(current parish)_ and your discernment with us.

Yours in Christ,
[name]
[Parish and committee name]

Tool 14a: Worksheet for Written Questions to Candidates

Subject area	Examples of questions[9]
Faith: What does the candidate believe? Why is he or she a priest? How does he or she live a life of faith day-to-day?	Please tell us how you were called to ministry, and tell us about your daily walk with Jesus Christ. Tell us about your spiritual journey and how that led you to apply for this position. Why are you an Episcopalian?
Worship	What are the underpinnings and components of meaningful worship experiences? *Clergy Ministry Portfolio question 2.*
Evangelism	How have you led your congregation into evangelism and outreach, and how might you apply this leadership in our parish? What are your passions in ministry?
Church growth by demographic such as age group, marital status and ethnicity	What do you see as keys to The Episcopal Church ministering to more young adults and young families? How have you acted on these where you are now? How have you achieved inclusiveness in your parish?

---

[9] Add your own ideas for questions. If the OTM Ministry Portfolio addresses this subject, its question is shown in italics.

Subject area	Examples of questions[9]
Stewardship of finances and facilities	What do you believe about stewardship of money and other resources?
	Please describe how you manage the annual fundraising process. Describe your best practices and your view of the respective roles of the rector, vestry, and stewardship committee.
	Please describe your experience with capital campaigns and endowments.
	Clergy Ministry Portfolio question 9.
Leadership/Vision	How have you helped your parish develop and achieve its vision?
	We believe you have extraordinary personal gifts to share during your years in full-time parish ministry, and we have unique gifts as a parish. What are your thoughts on pursuing a vision for ministry that would marry your gifts with ours?
	Clergy Ministry Portfolio questions 3, 7, and 11.
Pastoral care	What have been your most gratifying successes in pastoral care?
	What qualities provide the foundation for strong pastoral care for your congregation?
	What is your experience in addressing pastoral care issues related to mental health?
	Clergy Ministry Portfolio question 6.
Preaching	What makes great preaching? How do you do it?
	Please provide copies of or links to some of your sermons.

Subject area	Examples of questions[9]
Outreach	What outreach project are you most proud of and why? Have you led your current church to modify a longstanding outreach ministry? If so, why? How did you lead the change? What have been the results?
Involvement in the church and community	How have you developed relationships in your parish and community and with your local diocese? How have you been a leader in your diocese and the church? *Clergy Ministry Portfolio question 5.*
Management	Please describe your management style, with specific examples of how you have interacted with and supported clergy, staff, and laity. How have you typically organized clergy, staff, and lay leadership roles? How have you helped your team members develop their ministries?
Conflict and consensus	How are you a pastor to your entire congregation, including members who disagree with you on important matters? How have you led a congregation to consensus on a difficult issue? When have you chosen to invite support rather than consensus? Why? How did you do it? *Clergy Ministry Portfolio question 10.*
Personality	How would your friends describe you? How about parishioners who do not know you well? Please describe one of your most important role models and why he or she is your role model.

Subject area	Examples of questions[9]
Family	Please tell us about your family. What have you learned from your family?
Personal development	What preparations for ministry have been most valuable to your vocation thus far? When have you failed, and what did you learn from that experience? How have you continued to pursue personal and vocational growth? *Clergy Ministry Portfolio question 8.*
Self-care	How do you keep your center? What were the biggest challenges to this in the past two years? Please describe a representative week in your current role. *Clergy Ministry Portfolio question 4.*

Tool 14b: Data Fields of the OTM's Clergy Ministry Portfolio

This is the current form that most priests complete for the OTM to provide to parishes with clergy openings.

Priest, Since

Preferred Contact Information (address, email and phone numbers)

Current Compensation   Required for New Position   Negotiable   Healthcare Needed

Housing/Rectory   Housing/ Rectory Detail   Housing Required for

Education

Position Preferences (Rector, Chaplain, diocesan staff, etc.)

Open to Consider New Position

Work History and Skills

Other Contact Information

Date of Last Background Check   Company Performing Check   Diocese Requesting

Sermons Preached   Resources Created

Online References   What Others Have Written

Groups and Associations

Languages Written   Languages Spoken   Languages in Which You Are Able to Lead Worship

Essay questions

1. Describe a moment in your recent ministry that you recognize as one of success and fulfillment.
2. Describe your liturgical style and practice.
3. How do you practice incorporating others in ministry?
4. How do you care for your spiritual emotional and physical well being?
5. Describe your involvement in either the wider church or geographical community.
6. How do you engage in pastoral care for others?
7. Tell about a ministry project that exists because of your leadership. What was

---

your role in its creation? Who can be contacted?

8. How are you preparing yourself for the church of the future?

9. What is your personal practice of stewardship and how do you utilize it to influence your ministry in your worshipping community?

10. What is your experience of conflict involving the church? And what is your experience in addressing it?

11. What is your experience leading/addressing change in the church? When has it gone well? When has it gone poorly? And what did you learn?

Names of References:

- Bishop
- Diocesan Transition Minister
- Active Clergy
- Inactive Clergy
- Colleague in Church Governance
- Colleague in Church Governance
- Colleague in Ministry
- Colleague in Ministry

Tool 14c: Worksheet for First Interviews

Prepare the candidate: *Tell him or her in advance what to expect, such as how many people will be present and how the time will be structured. Our committee provided our warm-up question in advance.*

Opening: *Start with a prayer. Our committee led the opening prayer and told the candidates we would ask them to conclude the hour with a prayer. Introduce everyone in the room, on and off camera, before asking your first question.*

Subject area[10]	Examples of questions
Warm-up question to put the candidate at ease while setting a substantive tone	Tell us about a formative experience from your childhood. Tell us about a parent or grandparent. Tell us about someone who has been a mentor to you. Tell us about an early experience in your ministry that comes to mind often.
Faith: What does the candidate believe? Why is he or she a priest? How does he or she live a life of faith day-to-day?	*You may have follow-up questions to your candidates' written responses in this area that may fit better later in the interview after you have established rapport.*
Worship	Describe any changes you have made to your current parish's worship services or experiments you have tried.
Evangelism	What does your current congregation do best in evangelism?
Church growth with particular populations such as age group, ethnicity, or life experience	Describe the demographics and social characteristics of your current congregation. How would you like these to be different (or the same) in ten years?

---

[10] You will want to ask every candidate certain questions and you will have additional tailored questions for each candidate based on his or her file.

Subject area[10]	Examples of questions
Stewardship of finances and facilities	What has worked best for your parish when raising money for annual operations and for special purposes?
Leadership/vision	How would your past wardens describe your leadership? *You may have follow-up questions to your candidates' written responses in this area.*
Pastoral care	What are the main challenges to providing your current congregation the pastoral care they need? What pastoral roles are you most drawn to personally? Which are more challenging for you?
Preaching	Describe how you prepare your sermons. *You may want to ask a specific question about one of the candidate's recent sermons that you watched or heard online.*
Outreach	What outreach activities have been most rewarding to you and why?
Involvement in the church and community	*Ask the candidate to comment on one of the interesting activities on his or her resume or Clergy Ministry Portfolio.*
Management	How would your staff describe your approach to delegation?
Conflict and consensus	*You may have follow-up questions to your candidates' written responses in this area.*

Subject area[10]	Examples of questions
Personality	*This is hard to explore in an interview format. Our candidates and our committee had fun with a "lightning round" of short, fast questions that called for one-word responses. One reason we did this was because our parish has a reputation for the organization and structure our large size requires but we wanted to show we had an informal, fun side. All the candidates were quick-witted, and several times we laughed together when candidates paused and said, "I can't believe I just said that!"*
Family	*The suggested written questions for this topic also work well in interviews.*
Personal development	What has been your most valuable personal development experience of the past year?
Self care	Walk us through a typical week or what you wish were a typical week.
Personal traits such as humor, warmth, gravitas or humility	*Notice the moments when you are struck by personality traits so you can compare notes later with the rest of your committee.*

Wrap-up: *After the interview and the candidate's questions for you, tell the candidate when to expect to hear from you next, and remind him or her of how to contact you with any questions in the meantime. Close with a prayer.*

Tool 15: Candidate Visit Schedule

The downloadable version of this tool is more detailed and can be adapted for planning and managing the visit.

Time	Activity	Committee Members	Individual Member's Name
Remember to give the candidate and spouse quiet rest breaks alone.	*Before the visit, ask the candidate what he or she particularly would like to see.*	*Which committee members will participate in each activity? Give every member small-group time with the candidate and spouse.*	*Create a column showing each member's availability during each time slot. The free online polls at www.doodle.com make this easy to do. This matrix helps to schedule the visit and to make substitutions when someone's calendar changes.*
Sunday, 5:00 p.m.	Pick up at airport, check into hotel, and bring to dinner	Martha and John	
7:00 – 9:00 p.m.	Dinner at Luke's home	Full committee	
9:00 – 10:00 p.m.	Secret tour of church	Mary and John	
8:30 a.m.	Pick up at hotel	Luke	
8:45 a.m.	Breakfast and Bible Study at Mary's	Full committee	
10:30 a.m.	Tour residential neighborhoods	Martha and Luke	
And so forth…			

Tool 16: Form for Reference Interviews

Candidate _____ Date _____	Reference _____ Phone_____
"Thank you for talking with me. What would be helpful to know about our parish in order to have this conversation? How do you know (name)?"	
Light question to start the conversation. For example, "What are five words that describe him/her?" or, "What was your most memorable experience with him/her?"	
"What are the best things he or she has done for his or her current parish?"	
"What do you expect he/she will do if he or she stays there?"	
"Ideally, what do you or others wish the candidate or the parish could do?" Answers to this question help you understand both the situation and the priest.	
"Why do you think he or she might be interested in our parish?"	
"How would you describe his or her personality?"	
"What gives him or her stress? We all have something. How is it manifested?"	
"Tell me about his or her spouse." This prompt may also elicit comments on the family and family life.	
"What do you imagine he or she would be if not a priest?"	
"Who else would you recommend as a reference?" The point is to seek several useful perspectives. I would not contact these secondary references without asking the priest's permission.	

Tool 17: Mutual Expectations Worksheet

This tool will help you and your new rector to start a strong ministry partnership by articulating mutual expectations. In a sense the lay leaders will say, "This is how we have done things," and the new rector will share ministry practices that have worked well for him or her in other parishes. This Tool is meant as a discussion guide. You and your new rector can decide whether or how you would note the shared understandings that you reach.

Topic	Sample discussion prompts
Worship	What are the congregation's experiences and expectations regarding Rite I, Rite II, music, seasonal services, language deviations from the Book of Common Prayer, choreography of Communion, incense, and so forth? Does the new rector want to introduce certain new worship experiences?
Special services	Does the congregation expect anything in particular regarding other clergy duties such as baptisms, weddings, and funerals?
Rector's duties	What are the opinions of the incoming rector and of the congregation regarding duties that only the rector should perform?
Staffing	Ordained and lay staff compensation is the largest investment of most parishes. Does the new rector have questions at the start? Are there any people the congregation feels must always, or never, be on the staff?
Finances	How is annual fundraising conducted? Does it work well? What ideas does the new rector have to share at the start? How are church finances managed?
Clergy discretionary fund	Most parishes provide a fund that the rector, or all clergy on staff, may use for various purposes, including meeting confidential pastoral needs. Because such disbursements can be so sensitive, it is wise to establish rules for yours in a written vestry policy. Your diocese may have a policy regarding clergy discretionary funds.

Topic	Sample discussion prompts
Other rector expenses	A parish should reimburse travel and "business" expenses that the rector and other staff incur in performing their duties. Share your written policy and any unwritten expectations.
Facilities	What spaces have shaped the DNA of the congregation? How are facilities managed? What are the biggest maintenance concerns and what is the rector's role in addressing them?
Vestry and other lay leadership	Who chairs vestry meetings, and how are the agendas set? What are the essential lay leadership roles in key ministries?
Diocese and The Episcopal Church	What involvement in your diocese and the church do you expect of your rector?
Community	What is the parish's role in the community, and what community roles will its rector take?
School (if the parish has one)	How is the school governed and managed? What have been the roles of past rectors?
Rector health	How will the parish support the rector's physical, mental, and spiritual health? What are mutual expectations about work schedules and on-call responsibilities? What are the vacation and sabbatical policies? Do the rector and lay leaders expect the rector will have a spiritual adviser and go on retreats away from the congregation?
Ongoing support	What are the mutual expectations about how the rector and lay leaders will seek regular feedback from each other on the full range of possible issues?

Tool 18: Employment Terms Worksheet

Subject	Considerations
Overall compensation	What are the salaries of other clergy with comparable responsibilities and capabilities in your area? Be sure to understand these data comprehensively; other churches may have a different combination of salary and benefits than you contemplate.
Moving expenses	Typically, the new parish pays moving expenses. How much is reasonable?
Salary	What is appropriate for the new rector now versus when your partnership reaches full speed? Can you think of milestones that should trigger a compensation review? For a younger rector, how may the compensation change as he or she "grows into" the role?
Social Security taxes	Consider in light of total compensation.
Housing (rectory)	How is routine maintenance handled? Are any major maintenance needs expected? Who will pay for utilities? If the rectory is used for parish events, are the set-up and cleanup handled by the church janitorial staff?
Housing (other)	If the rector buys a house, will the church assist with brokerage fees and closing costs? Will the church provide assistance with the down payment or mortgage payments?
Healthcare	What insurance plan does the parish have for clergy and lay staff? What known healthcare needs does the rector have? Since the health insurance system is so complex, can the parish help introduce the rector to medical providers who will be covered?
Re-creation	Rectors are in a sense "on call" 24/7, but plan for the rector to have two scheduled days off every week. Plan for paid vacations that include Sundays away. Your parish should have a sabbatical policy.

Subject	Considerations
Other support	What does the rector need? How can the parish help meet these needs, financially and otherwise? What would he or she appreciate and benefit from, such as a club or museum membership?
Intellectual property	Address ownership of teaching content, social media pages, and other content the rector generates while employed by the parish.

Tool 19: Announce the New Rector

Task	Who is responsible?	Timing	Notes
Announce to the rector's current parish that he or she is leaving. This is the first priority because their transition began when the rector first talked with you, and now will accelerate.	New rector, together with his or her bishop. Their list of steps will determine the timing of some of your steps.	Set the hours to tell the wardens and vestry in person, followed by the parish via email and by a simultaneous announcement on the website and social media sites.	State in the first communication exactly when the rector will leave and whatever is known about how the transition will unfold.
Make a detailed plan to share your news with stakeholders as follows:	Wardens and search chair(s).	Before the rector accepts your call.	Apprise your bishop of the plan.
Interim rector.	Senior warden.	Immediately.	Agree on the date of the interim rector's last Sunday and last day and on the date when the employment agreement notice period will be triggered for compensation purposes.
Your church's other clergy.	Senior warden.	Almost immediately.	

Task	Who is responsible?	Timing	Notes
Other staff.	Senior warden.	In person, simultaneously with the announcement to the congregation.	Recognize their fear of changes that could hurt their employment.
Congregation.	Depends on parish communications systems.	Do not start before the rector's former congregation knows. For large churches this delay applies to the staff as well.	Use email. Simultaneously announce on the website and social media sites. Tell in the first communication when the new rector will start. Provide photos and a brief biography. Churches with high-quality video capabilities could consider producing a video with the new rector, but few churches can make an energetic high quality video under such time pressure.

Task	Who is responsible?	Timing	Notes
Lay leaders.	Search committee members can do this best because they know the new rector personally.	Concurrent with the announcement to the congregation.	It is easy to add individual cover notes to the parish-wide email to personalize your messaging to and build excitement among the lay leaders. When someone mentions the new rector to a fellow parishioner, you want him or her to say, "Yes, I heard from _____, and the new rector sounds great for us!"
Community.	Depends on parish communications systems.	Within two days of announcing to the congregation.	Provide a press release to local media with a photo of the new rector.
Former clergy.	Wardens and search chair(s).	Concurrent with the announcement to the congregation.	Send a note to past rectors and other clergy, and give them and the new rector each other's contact information.
Diocesan clergy.	Bishop.	Your bishop will determine how to introduce your new rector and to other diocesan clergy.	Ask if the bishop needs anything beyond a copy of your announcements to the congregation.

Task	Who is responsible?	Timing	Notes
Notice the questions people ask.	Vestry and search committee.	Less than a week after announcing.	Expect parishioners will promptly visit the rector's former church's website and access sermons there. Compare questions that each of you hears from members of the congregation. If the same questions recur, update the website announcement to address them.

Tool 20: Welcome

Activity	Who is responsible?	Timing	Notes
Coordinate the rector's move.			
Plan the rector's departure from his or her previous location.	Rector and spouse.	Start immediately after the call is accepted.	Much depends on whether he or she must sell a house.
Provide for a vacation before the rector arrives.	Senior warden.		Provide time for the new rector to recharge between leaving his or her previous parish and joining you.
Give orientation packages to the rector and his or her family members.	Designate parishioners.		Include material on local history and attractions and a list of websites for local media and services. Provide age-appropriate gifts for his or her family. (Creative members of our Dallas search committee gave cowboy boots to our rector's young children.)
Ask about the interests, favorite foods, etc., of each family member.	Designate parishioners.		Use this insight to plan orientation tours for the family and to stock their pantry.

Activity	Who is responsible?	Timing	Notes
Assist the rector with purchasing a home, if this is your system.	Parishioners can help with practical matters, for example, introductions to realtors, mortgage bankers, and others.		Consider making a bridge loan. Few priests have enough equity to purchase a new home before the previous one sells.
Prepare the rectory if you have one.	The vestry can appoint people to oversee this activity.		Arrange the current inhabitant's move-out. Inspect, schedule maintenance, refresh paint, and make any necessary repairs.
Prepare for the arrival.			
Assist with physical moving and house set-up.	Designate a parishioner to coordinate each activity.		Be available, but do not overwhelm them.
Provide local information.			Include a map and lists of stores for groceries, pharmaceuticals, clothing, hobby supplies, etc.
Organize meals for the first few days.			Make the deliveries unobtrusive, such as leaving baskets on the doorstep.

Activity	Who is responsible?	Timing	Notes
Arrange a school tour if the rector has children.			Contact and include the school principal.
Provide information on doctors, dentists, and other medical providers.			Offer personal introductions and provide a copy of the medical insurance Summary of Benefits.
Lead local tours.			Personalize tours for every family member. Children will appreciate finding the ice cream shop.
Celebrate as a congregation.			
Schedule a formal New Rector Institution Service.	Designate a parishioner to coordinate this service, and involve your bishop in the planning.	Hold this event within a few weeks of your rector's arrival. Include a reception and meal events for visitors.	Plan a memorable service officially marking the beginning of your rector's ministry with you, based on the liturgy in the Book of Common Prayer (page 559). Invite a mentor or friend of the new rector as guest preacher. Invite the rector's old friends and extended family.

Activity	Who is responsible?	Timing	Notes
Plan the first week and first Sunday.	Rector and a designated parishioner.	Set the dates immediately when the rector accepts your call, and advertise it in your announcement.	Set the rector's start date the week before the first Sunday so that he/she gets to know the staff and rhythms of the parish. Make the first Sunday celebratory, energizing, and warm, and include a welcome reception.
Invite people personally to the rector's first Sunday.	All lay leaders.		Every congregation has visitors who are not quite engaged and former parishioners who have drifted away. Use this moment to invite them. The most effective invitation is delivered by the voice of a friend.
Plan the next few Sundays.	Rector.		Consider a sermon series that makes worshippers want to come back next week. Consider a teaching series based on the season or something that emphasizes a unique ministry of the parish.
Make a digital photographic album of the welcome events.	Many will take photos. Have a parishioner collect them and do quick on-screen editing.		Post highlights on Facebook, Instagram, and other social media and on parish bulletin boards.

Tool 21: Orientation

Activity	Who is responsible?	Timing	Notes
Make a set of orientation files.			
History and lore of the parish	Designate a parishioner.	These files can be assembled during interim period.	Include the chronology and events that have shaped the DNA of the parish.
List of all deaths in the parish in the past five years			Include deaths of parishioners' extended families. Note deaths that were particularly traumatic for any reason.
Local and regional history, geography and lore			Could include books, brochures, Chamber of Commerce material, etc.
List of local religious institutions and their leaders			
Parish Service Register			This register is kept as required to record attendance and other information needed to complete the Parochial Report every parish is required to provide its diocese soon after the end of each calendar year.
Directory of parishioner phones, email, and physical addresses			

Activity	Who is responsible?	Timing	Notes
Vestry calendar			Include notes on when various issues typically are covered during the year.
Copy of the book of vestry minutes			
Parish corporate formation documents and by-laws	Chancellor		
Parish financial records	Treasurer		Include income statements for the past five to ten years, the current balance sheet and records of any other funds. The objective is not to make the rector a CPA but to demystify the finances and to inform. Most rectors need a personal orientation from the treasurer.
All written policies of the parish	Chancellor		
Human resources files and any written job descriptions			
Wedding and funeral planning booklets			
Any written orientation material of parish organizations			These might include the Altar Guild, choir, youth leaders, and so forth.

Activity	Who is responsible?	Timing	Notes
Names and dates of visiting preachers and speakers in past five years			
Newsletters, worship bulletins, and parish-wide communications, back to at least a year before the previous rector left			
All hymnals and other worship materials the parish uses			
Written records on facilities	The rector should not be the facility manager.		Compile contact information for contractors, for example, the HVAC maintenance company.
Prepare the rector's office.			
Set up a computer and private printer.			
Clean windows and carpets and refresh paint.			
Make a full set of church keys.			
Help the rector start relationships.			
Nametags			Have every parishioner wear nametags at church.

Activity	Who is responsible?	Timing	Notes
Introduce former vestry and other parish leaders.		In the first six weeks. (Large parishes need longer.)	Arrange group dinners for all former vestry and other parish leaders to meet the rector.
Coordinate with parish ministry groups.			Every group should include the rector in one of its next regular meetings. This could include outreach committees, prayer groups, book clubs, and so forth.
Arrange small-group gatherings of parishioners.			Schedule informal social gatherings where any parishioner can meet the new rector.
Help the rector start community relationships.			
Tour local hospitals and assisted living centers.			Visit those sites where the rector may make pastoral visits. Engage leaders of these institutions.
Make community introductions.			Ask parishioners to host lunches or breakfasts with community leaders.
Highlight certain clubs and cultural institutions.	—		Introduce the rector to institutions that are important to parishioners, for example, museums, local clubs, and so forth.

Tool 22: Project Management Worksheet

Create a worksheet based on the example. Create columns as shown below for (1) Description and Notes, (2) Leader, (3) Participants, (4) Planned Start Date, and (5) Estimated Finish Date. When identifying participants, be sure to distinguish between vestry and search committee roles. After you fill in the worksheet, you can sort by different columns to see these activities by leader or start or completion date. To add more detailed activities, simply insert rows.

Activity	(1)	(2)	(3)	(4)	(5)
Develop a parish prayer for the transition.					
Study church transition concepts.					
Discuss the transition with the bishop or diocesan transition minister.					
Plan the Ending Stage of the transition with the outgoing rector.					
Celebrate the Ending Stage.					
Establish strategy for ongoing communications with the congregation throughout the transition.					
Engage an interim rector.					
Organize congregational discussions about the parish and the transition.					
Assess the parish and imagine the future.					
Establish lay committee(s) to lead the rector transition and search.					
Launch the search committee in a way that sets the stage for spiritual discernment.					
Develop search committee plan for confidentiality.					

Activity	(1)	(2)	(3)	(4)	(5)
Schedule a retreat for the search committee to bond deeply.					
Study the role of a rector.					
Agree on qualities we seek in our rector.					
Complete parish profile.					
Complete OTM "Ministry Portfolio."					
Complete "Open Positions Form" if diocese is in the Transition Ministry Conference.					
Study spiritual discernment together.					
Agree on discernment process.					
Identify prospective candidates by sharing parish profile and inviting suggestions.					
Write summaries of prospective candidates.					
Invite prospects to become candidates.					
Collect application material.					
Review candidate information.					
Hold discernment discussions.					
Complete initial teleconference interviews.					
Continue discernment discussions.					
Host candidate visits.					
Continue discernment discussions.					
Visit candidates.					
Continue discernment discussions.					
Interview candidate references.					

Activity	(1)	(2)	(3)	(4)	(5)
Obtain background check.					
Engage in final discernment.					
Discuss mutual expectations.					
Agree on employment terms.					
Announce!					
Welcome the new rector.					
Help the new rector become oriented.					
(Insert activities to strengthen the ministry partnership with the rector.)					
Create a sealed file for successors.					
Share our insights with other parishes.					

Made in the USA
Middletown, DE
14 June 2023

32578887R00099